That Girl's in a Wheelchair

That Girl's in a Wheelchair

Shalida A. Askanazi

Open Waters Publishing
(an imprint of The Pilgrim Press)
1300 East 9th Street
Cleveland, Ohio 44114
thepilgrimpress.com

Published 2026.

Library of Congress Cataloging-in-Publication Data on file.
LCCN: 2025941429

ISBN 978-0-8298-1045-5 (paper)
ISBN 978-0-8298-1964-9 (ebook)

Typeset in Baskerville, Mr. Eaves, and Mynerve.

Printed on acid-free paper in the United States of America.

To anyone who needs a reminder that no dream is too big, the best person to bet on is yourself, and being sensitive is a superpower.

Mom, you're the strongest person I know.

Introduction

Early in our relationship, for our first vacation together, Cory and I went to Put-in-Bay. While exploring the island we stopped at a bar for a drink. We still talk about the trip years later, but one moment at this bar still bothers us both. The hostess asked us if we were there for the bar. We replied yes. I've never been to a bar that was wheelchair accessible. I'm short and would never be able to reach the bar. We asked the hostess if we could have a table since I couldn't reach the bar. She said no. We were both nervous about handling this situation because we were only a couple of months into our relationship. The two of us are also very non-confrontational, so we ended up walking until we found a place that would serve us. I was too embarrassed to bring it up, and Cory could tell I didn't want to talk about it, but I could see that he was upset that I was treated that way.

A few months later, on a trip to Target, as we browsed the aisles for homewares, we passed a mother, father, and son who appeared to be about eight or nine. He looked up at me, pointed his finger at my chair, and said, "That girl's in a wheelchair!" I ignored him because, after years of experiencing it, I didn't want to acknowledge the embarrassment. But as soon as we were far from the family, Cory turned to me and looked really upset.

"Yeah, I know," I said. I already knew his thoughts.

"The parents should've told that kid it's impolite to point at people," he said.

"Yeah, they should've."

"They just stood there and didn't say anything," he went on to say.

"I guess I'm just used to it."

The rage Cory felt was completely valid. I spent many years prior feeling the same way. I think Cory's own physical disability made him understand how I felt. With his Eagle Barretts Syndrome, his stomach protrudes out since he doesn't have stomach muscles. It's noticeable and he gets self-conscious, especially when buying clothes. He had so many surgeries as a child, just like me, and had a hard time fitting in, just like me. We both navigated our childhood trying not to stand out even though we had noticeable physical differences from our peers. Once we got in the car, he looked at me and said, "Sorry for being so grumpy; I just think parents should correct that behavior."

"I completely agree, so when we have kids, we'll make sure they never unintentionally make someone uncomfortable."

Growing up, I always envisioned myself as one of the bombshells on those 1960s pulp fiction book covers. You know, the ones where a woman is running away from a haunted castle in a glamorous curve-hugging slip dress, a full face of makeup, and hair that screams *seductress*. She's probably running away from a ghost or vampire, and in bold letters on the cover, the title is something straightforward like, "She's Dead." Picture the cover of *The Family at Tammerton* by Margaret Erskine. I saw myself as a book cover heroine trying to get away from the strangers who were pointing and saying rude things about my wheelchair. If I'm going to think about these situations, I might as well envision myself as a glam goddess.

As the months went on, the incident slowly turned into an inside joke between me and Cory. Going around the house, we would say to each other, "That girl's in a wheelchair!" We would laugh, and after a while, the embarrassment from the encounter disappeared. I learned at a young age to keep my head up high and not to make eye contact with people even when they were staring at me. As an adult, my favorite thing to do is to toss on a pair of dark sunglasses and cosplay as an uninterested celebrity ignoring the paparazzi (whatever it takes to deal with assholes). When trying to develop a title for this book, I thought long and hard about what I wanted to name it. In true poet fashion, I wanted something deep and moody. I wanted a title that stood out to generations of people, like the late Elizabeth Wurtzel's *Prozac Nation*.

I didn't think I was important enough to write a memoir. Truthfully, all I know is that my story isn't wholly unique. There are other Black disabled women who probably grew up in the inner city, experienced abuse, and somehow made it. I guess the significant difference is that there's only one me, and my story may be familiar, but it's definitely not the same as others. The most crucial difference is that I get to tell my story, and only I write these words. Each chapter of this memoir is just a snapshot of my life.

I always wanted to help the world heal with my words, and I still hold that goal close to me. Maybe the whole world won't be healed, but maybe one person will read this book and feel heard and seen. Sometimes, being acknowledged is all we need to pull through. I also want to mention that I have no hard feelings toward the kid who pointed at me in Target, or his parents. Maybe this book can be used for education, though I don't believe it's my job to educate people on how to be decent humans. As much as the disabled community gets stared at, you would think people would have a genuine interest in the things we need to survive in this world. Instead, we're under a microscope and ignored at the same time. We are completely left behind in the conversation of equality; we can't legally marry or save more than two thousand dollars without losing Medicaid health insurance. With popular Black disabled activists like Imani Barbarin and Keah Brown, I hope our experiences reach a larger audience.

I'm writing this book in my early thirties. I plan on having a lot more life ahead of me, and if I manage to get another book deal for a memoir, I hope you'll read it to see the growth. Because that's really all we're doing in life, right? Growing and becoming whoever we want to become. I would also like to point out that there is no secret potion in this book to help you figure out who you're supposed to be. It's one of those things that just comes with living life. Experiencing the good and the bad and finding a gem in each of them. Throughout my life, I've gone through a lot of bad things, but after a distance from the situation, I find the lessons in them. It's not easy to do, and I still have a hard time with it, but finding the lessons makes me feel a whole lot lighter.

My Religion

When my family had trouble paying rent, we would always go back to my granny's apartment. She lived in a brick building in the Collinwood neighborhood of Cleveland with four rental units on top. My granny and grandpa were the tenants who had lived there the longest. My grandpa's coworker also lived in one of the units. He eventually became my stepfather, and my mom, my brother, and I moved into another unit with him in that same building. I could play in between our apartment and my grandparents' apartment, grab a snack from granny, and go home for dinner. When money got tight, all four of us moved into my grandparents' place. On Sundays, we would wake up to the loud thundering of drums and cymbals emanating from the Baptist church on the building's ground floor. The choir would be belting out gospel music, the congregation stomping and clapping along. There was no way to sleep in. Trust me, I tried. We never visited the church, but we were always polite with the pastor. We weren't religious, but we celebrated Easter and Christmas (mainly to have an excuse to cook big meals and get the family together).

My favorite part about the church below us was that I could sit perched on the back of the couch and look out the window to see the parade of churchgoers: Little girls like me in frilly white dresses, older women in sherbet-colored outfits and giant hats I had never seen my granny wear, men and boys in suits and shiny shoes. Everyone looked so put together and happy. Everyone looked like a real family. I would tell myself that those kids probably didn't live in a two-bedroom apartment with their grandparents, mom, stepdad, and newborn brother. Sometimes another kid would spot me looking from the window, and I would duck, embarrassed.

"We just aren't church people; church doesn't make people perfect," I remember my granny saying. For us, Sundays were for coupon clipping, watching football, doing laundry, and cooking a big meal that would give us enough leftovers for the upcoming week. However, I did go to church once with my grandpa and cousins. Grandpa really wanted to take all the granddaughters to the Easter church service. Our granny and my mom braided and straightened everyone's hair the night before. The final additions were to add beads and top our little heads off with straw hats to match our dresses. I was excited because I finally had the chance to wear a frilly white dress and shiny shoes. Each of us even got a little white patent leather handbag to carry. Before leaving, Granny sprayed us with her favorite perfume. Ironically, we didn't go to the church that was right below us—we went around the corner. Grandpa pushed me in my wheelchair as my three cousins marched in front of us.

Once we made it to the crowded church, we saw we weren't the only little Black girls dressed in their Sunday best. We went inside and sat through the sermon. My shoes started to feel too tight, and the beads were click-clacking too loudly when I moved my head. I just wanted to get home to eat my Easter candy and have Easter dinner. We finally left, and that was the last time I went to church for Easter. As I got older, I noticed the amount of people visiting the church downstairs became sparse. Sunday mornings were a lot quieter without the instruments and choir. I remember overhearing my grandparents say that the pastor was having an affair and every night his mistress would park her car right outside the church. I also remember hearing that the pastor began sleeping in the church instead of going home.

Throughout the rest of my childhood, and though we were not religious, I would say my prayers every night. It became a part of my ritual to ensure nothing bad would happen the following day. I grew from saying the childhood "now I lay me down to sleep" prayer to saying a lengthy prayer that consisted of naming each person of my family, which took a long time since I included extended members; by the time I was finished my eyes would shut automatically from exhaustion. If for some reason I forgot to pray the night before, I had to do it in the morning.

One day I asked my mom if she could get me a children's Bible. She was confused since we never went to church, but she figured asking for a Bible wasn't the worst thing. In middle school, I became friends with the girls who got made fun of for being "super-Christian good girls." I begged my mom to let me go to church with my best friend from the group, Alisha. One morning Alisha handed me a thin silver ring. I asked what it was for, and she said, "it's a promise ring—to stay a virgin until you're married." When I got home to show my mom, I could tell she was uncomfortable just from seeing her confused look. Plus, she hadn't talked to me about sex yet. I wonder if she felt attacked since she was a teenage mother. She also started to notice how obsessive I was becoming. At this point, she was a single mom with a preteen who had obvious mental health issues and a little kid who was always on her hip. I don't think she really knew what to do about me. Looking back, the easiest solution would have been to put me in therapy, but my mom had a fear of asking for help.

After middle school, Alisha and I went to different high schools, but her church continued to mail me flyers. One flyer was just a photo of the pastor and a handwritten note on the back expressing how much he enjoyed me being there and hoped I would come back to the church. Truthfully, I didn't see the harm in it then, but now I understand why my protective mother freaked out and told me I couldn't go back to that church. In her eyes, the flyer was creepy. One other incident happened at a church in Cleveland that we were invited to by a neighbor. I wore a denim skirt and as the service went on, one of the older women laid a white sheet over my lap and chastised me about how the men in the church were looking up my skirt, and I should know better. I was thirteen. About a week later, the cheap silver promise ring I wore everyday broke, I asked my mom for a replacement, and she said no. I asked why, and she told me she was sick of Christians and their judgmental ways.

For the sake of being cool in high school, I dropped the Christian girl personality, and honestly, Christianity wasn't clicking with me during that time, especially witnessing many self-righteous church-people firsthand. Growing up, my family didn't judge people for how they identified themselves, and I had questions about how hateful some takes from Christianity seemed. I began going to the Cleveland School of the Arts and made so many friends who were a part of the LGBTQIA+ community, a community I was becoming a part of; I also started to notice that I was developing feelings for girls like I did for boys. Even though religion wasn't something I wanted to identify with anymore, saying my nightly prayers was still something I needed to do. My obsessive compulsive disorder was out of control—I was having intrusive thoughts that made me afraid of what I could do to myself, and my depression was just as bad if not worse. Praying is what my brain felt like I needed to do to make sure nothing bad happened, but in my freshman year of college, I stopped praying. By that point, so many bad things already happened to us: food insecurity, homelessness, and overall abuse. I realized that praying didn't solve anything for me or prevent anything from happening to me. It also no longer gave me comfort.

I took this opportunity to learn about more other religions. I got into Wicca around the age of twenty; looking back, it was a way to rebel. I loved it, and I felt like a badass practicing a religion I thought was so cool. I even got my brother, River, who was growing into a very outspoken and progressive teen, into Wicca, and later my mom even became interested in it. For the first time in my life, I felt like I was part of something bigger. It helped to have friends at my university who were also getting into Wicca, because I felt less alone. We bonded by doing spells and reading books and tarot cards. Somedays we would meet for coffee and discuss the knowledge we were getting from studying the new-to-us religion. We all had a trauma-filled relationship with Christianity, which is why Wicca appealed to us; we felt like Wicca was a way for us to heal. Friends knew the perfect gifts to give me—tarot cards, crystals, and any book that had spells in it. I didn't realize how lonely I was, and for the first time, I felt like I had a community, like I belonged somewhere.

As I got older and really took the time to research Wicca, I realized it was something I no longer wanted to be involved with. The stealing from Indigenous groups didn't sit right with me. I didn't want to contribute to the harm of those communities. I wasn't the only one. I noticed around this time that my other Black friends decided to quit as well. It sucked not having that community anymore, but I decided I should start looking into my own culture and what my ancestors practiced. I looked more into African American spirituality. I learned that things I grew up doing with my family were parts of Hoodoo. As children, the elders in our family always told us to burn the hair that was in our combs and brushes because a witch could get ahold of it and use it to punish you, or a bird could get it to use in its nest, and you would "lose your mind." Another practice that had Hoodoo origins was that you should never put your purse on the floor; you'll lose money fast. I was enthralled with the history of the Orishas and setting up an altar; I took an interest in Oshun, who is a part of the Yoruba religion and is associated with fertility and love. My brother was getting into it too, and we bonded over it. It made me feel closer to my ancestors. I felt safe, like I had a blanket of protection from those who came before me. I again felt like I belonged somewhere. Other friends started to take an interest as well and when Beyoncé released the *Lemonade* album it seemed like every Black person wanted to learn more about the Orishas and African spirituality. I loved that my community was learning about our ancestors and building that connection that was so violently ripped from us.

After meeting my now husband, Cory, I started to learn more about his family. His paternal grandfather was a Holocaust survivor who fixed shoes for a Nazi. He did this after pleading for his life; the Nazi told him that he would die if he didn't fix them correctly. Despite fixing the shoes, the Nazis still sent him away to a death march. The survivors of the march were later saved and sent to America. My husband's grandfather opened a shoe repair business in America and remarried after losing his whole family in the Holocaust. Unbeknownst to the family, he was also squirreling away money just in case the Nazis came back for him. His story touched me. I didn't know much about Judaism, but I was curious. Even though my husband identifies as Jewish, he's agnostic. His whole family is filled with scientists and doctors, so everyone has a scientific outlook on the world. But they hold being Jewish very close.

At one Thanksgiving, I asked my mother-in-law about her experience converting to Judaism after meeting my father-in-law.

She said that after hearing the family story, she felt like she had no choice. I agreed. With everything the family went through, it seemed essential to keep the tradition going. That is when I decided I would convert to Judaism. I interviewed different rabbis and researched the process. There would be a lot of learning, but I was completely down to do it. My husband would have married me regardless of whether I converted. For him, it wasn't a big deal. But I wanted to ensure that, if we had children, they would be Jewish. I enjoyed learning about Judaism and loved how a big part of the religion was to question everything. I remember, as a kid, questioning many things in Christianity but would have never said those things out loud. But with Judaism, that was encouraged. However, with the stress of my mom's declining mental health and setting boundaries with her, I stopped contacting rabbis and fell into a deep depression.

One day my husband asked why I hadn't been doing any of my "witchy stuff," referring to my Hoodoo. I could tell he was concerned about my mental health. I shrugged my shoulders and said I just hadn't wanted to do anything. I was depressed and took no interest in anything. He was right; I completely abandoned the altar I set up for my ancestors and wasn't studying any Judaism. He asked if I was upset that he wouldn't go to classes with me at the synagogue or try to build a relationship with the Jewish community in our city. I told him no. I already knew he wasn't religious, and I would never ask him to do something he wasn't comfortable with. This journey was mine alone.

When I was a kid looking out of the window at the families going into the church, it wasn't the religion I wanted, but the sense of structure and community. I love stability and feel content and safe with my living environment for the first time in my life. I don't have to worry about food insecurity or homelessness. I still have anxiety and OCD; I go to therapy for those things now, and I'm medicated. This is also the first time in my life that I don't feel the need to identify as any religion. I kind of do my own thing spiritually. Some days I'll read parts of the Torah and other Jewish literature; I'm also doing some Hoodoo work with my spiritual advisor. I took down my altar because I noticed my OCD began to get too intertwined with it. I recently found a TikTok account called Jewitches, and I've been falling in love with the knowledge they share and how they intertwine Judaism and witchcraft. One plus side to trying so many religions is that I've picked up so much knowledge. I have always loved learning, even if I don't stick with something. Maybe one day I'll put the altar back up, but for now, I'm satisfied. I don't think one belief is more perfect than another. I also won't say that one treats people better than the other. I believe every religion is flawed, and that's okay. We shouldn't seek perfection.

If someone asked me right now what I believed in, I would tell them I believe that the universe is so large, there's so much we don't know. I would tell them, everything doesn't always have an answer. I would tell them, I believe in whatever makes me feel safe.

Tangerine Sun

We've fallen so deep so fast
Straight into the Euphrates
Arms flailing like a hummingbird
tasting the sweetest nectar
We've pushed against the currents
Turquoise water rushes by
River rocks beneath our feet
Grappling for a moment of peace
A moment of air
The sight of the tangerine sun
Beaming down on us
To lift us up
To be a guiding light
Then it settles
We're now still
Like a hummingbird on a branch
Cherishing a full belly
Content with the outcome
Surviving another day
Tossed into the river

My River

I will not use my brother's deadname in this chapter, and I will only use the pronouns she/her for their past before they came out as trans; anything after will be either they or he. The only name I will be using is their chosen name, River. It's so important to respect and protect our trans loved ones, especially in this hateful society where their lives are so easily disregarded.

Up until the age of six, I was the only child. My mom said she was afraid to get pregnant again because she was worried that another baby would be born disabled like me. That changed when she met my future stepdad. They quickly started dating and eventually married. Soon thereafter, my mom became pregnant.

I had cousins to play with, but other than that, I was a very lonely child. At night I would wish for a sister so I could have a playmate. It didn't dawn on me that there would be an age gap and that we might not get along. I just knew I didn't want to be alone. When my mom told me she was pregnant, she sat on our couch in our tiny one-bedroom apartment and said she needed to get milk from our neighbor Mr. Whitaker, an elderly man who gave my mom rides and sometimes babysat me. I asked why, and she said she needed to drink milk because she was having a baby and needed extra calcium. I was ecstatic, and eventually, my mom gave birth to a little girl with the biggest cheeks and the curliest black hair. She named her after her father and me by combining both our names, going against my suggestion of Kate, the youngest sister of the cartoon character Arthur Reed who I watched religiously on PBS.

I loved staring at the new baby and hated going to school and being away from her. She was my real-life baby doll, and I felt like her protector. One day in speech therapy, I got so frustrated because I couldn't figure out how to say my R's correctly and just wanted to be home with my new sister that I started to cry hysterically. I was in the first grade, and my teacher told me I shouldn't cry because I was too old for that now.

Soon after the birth of the baby my mom and stepfather began getting into physical fights. Sometimes he would threaten to pour her insulin down the drain, and she would bite him in retaliation. Other times they would be on the floor wrestling. When this happened, I would sit on the bed with my baby sister as she sat in her car seat, upset, and I would turn her away from the fight and play pattycake with her until she laughed with her gummy mouth. After she calmed down, I would go to my grandparents' apartment next door and tell them my mom and stepfather were fighting. This became a regular routine for me. I was on edge all the time and started having trouble sleeping. I felt I always needed to be on high alert to protect the baby. My worst fear was that they would fight so wildly and accidentally fall on her.

After my stepfather had an affair, they divorced. My baby sister was three and attached to our mother; she also developed a bad habit of scratching me with her little but surprisingly sharp nails. As our six-year age gap became more prominent in our relationship, we argued and fought all the time. To me, she was an annoying kid sister, and to her, I was a bossy older sister. The fighting got so bad that our mom took us to our pediatrician, who told our mom that eventually we'd stop fighting, but that the age gap made us "incompatible." Technically we're half-siblings because we have different fathers. But if anyone asked, neither one of us would use the term half-sister or half-sibling, and as much as we fought, we always stood up for one another when one of us would get in trouble. So many times, I remember her screaming to our mom, "Leave my sister alone!"

As the years went on, we eventually began to get along. Especially once I left for college. In my freshman year, I was eighteen and trying to figure out how to navigate college on my own in Pennsylvania. My mom and sister were struggling with money and housing. At one point my mom met a random guy in line for government heating assistance. I instantly disliked him, but I couldn't figure out why. My mom ended up moving in with him, along with my sister. My grandmother and I decided to research this guy, and we found out that he was a registered sex offender. I was furious at my mom for putting my sister at risk. I remember calling her and telling her how stupid she was. It's not something I'm proud of but I was a scared teenager trying to protect not only my sister but my mother too. She later told me she moved in with him because she wanted to make sure she had a reliable way to visit me in Pennsylvania since he had a car and didn't mind making the drive.

I began coming up with ideas on how to get custody of my sister, mainly by researching resources online. I had no money, was living in a college dorm, and had no idea how to raise anyone, but my eighteen-year-old-self thought it couldn't be too hard. I eventually let that dream go but promised myself to keep a lookout for any dangerous situations my mom might put herself and my sister in. As our mom's mental health continued to decline, her outbursts became more frequent. When I came for Christmas, during my first year of college, we had no food or money for gifts. I told my little sister we could decorate the house with homemade decorations. She was twelve, and I was happy I could cheer her up. We made snowflakes and gingerbread men out of paper. I was doing fashion blogging and had money left over from a sponsorship I had done with a well-known soap brand. I used that last bit of money to get my sister some items from her favorite store. Nothing expensive because I think I only had about twenty dollars to spare.

When Christmas day came, I felt proud that I was able to bring some cheer to the house we were living in. My mom had been in a bad mood all week and did nothing but sleep on the couch. When she wasn't sleeping, she was lashing out at us for little things. I went to the living room to wake her and ask if she wanted to watch River open her gifts. She got up from the couch, got in my face, and screamed, "I don't give a fuck what she does!" I was startled but grabbed the gift bag I made for River and let her open everything; she was happy, but I could see the fear on her face from mom's outburst. Soon we heard mom storming through the house ripping our decorations off the walls and screaming. I didn't know what to do, so I sat there frozen in fear and sadness. I didn't care that I hadn't gotten any gifts, it wasn't a big deal to me because I had gotten used to it in the last few years. I wanted to make sure River had a somewhat normal holiday, but mom just had to ruin it.

Situations like this continued often, and we learned to stay out of mom's way. However, in one incident, I couldn't stand back and watch. Mom's mental health issues made her believe that people were coming into the house and replacing her family photos with photos she had never seen before. This went on for about a week; she talked about lasers being pointed at us as we slept. I was maybe twenty-three or twenty-four and was letting her use my disability check as her income. By this time, I already dropped out of college to focus on my mental health and was ready to move my life in a better direction. On this particular day, I was in the kitchen when I heard River crying in her room. Mom was screaming at River, accusing her of letting people into the house to replace family photos. I could hear River crying and sobbing that she didn't know what mom was talking about. Mom was yelling, "Tell me the truth, who are you working with!" I rushed into the room and saw River sitting on her bed in tears as Mom stood over her pointing and shouting.

"Get away from her," I yelled.

Mom ran towards me and got in my face, pointing her finger. "You're the reason River is working against me!"

"I don't know what you're talking about, but you're not going to talk to River this way."

It was the first time I really stood up to my mother. She went straight to the living room and slept on the couch for the rest of the day. The next week she dragged River and me to her therapist's office. She told us that if we weren't going to be honest with her, we would have to be honest in front of a professional because she knew we were working with people to add different family photos around the house. As I sat in the cramped office, I looked over at mom, she had the biggest smile on her face. I could tell she felt she won. My mom had been seeing this therapist for about six months. I don't remember for what, but it wasn't for the schizophrenia I thought could be the reason for her behavior; I don't think the therapist saw the signs. As the therapist listened to the story, she took a deep breath and looked mom straight in the eye and said, "These girls aren't lying, I've been doing this for a long time, and I know when people lie to me, but these girls have no idea what you're talking about." I saw the frustration on mom's face. She thought she was right. She thought we were working with people to confuse or trick her. As we left the appointment, neither of us spoke to each other. We just waited for the bus in silence. A few days later mom and I went to grab a few groceries from the store up the road. She stopped me and got on her knee on the sidewalk and through tears grabbed my hands and said, "Shalida, please tell me who's putting the photos in the house and the lasers," she begged.

"Mom, get up."

"Shalida, please don't give up on me. Promise you won't give up on me."

"Okay, Mom."

Then we continued to the store like nothing happened. A week later, she was back to accusing us of helping people plant photos around the house and point lasers at her.

Now that River and I are both adults and both living on our own, I think about little Shalida wishing on a star and asking for a sibling to be her best friend, and she got just that. I know I'm incredibly blessed to have the relationship I have with River because many people never get that. At times I do have to remind myself that I don't need to be a "mom" to River, they need me as their big sister, and that's more than enough. Knowing that I have my River by my side for the rest of my life makes everything I went through worth it. Even if you are an only child, I hope you have someone who is your River.

So Easy to Hurt Me

Content Warning: This chapter deals with sensitive topics including sexual abuse and suicide.

When I was fourteen and in ninth grade, I remember seeing this boy at school. He was wearing a vintage Nirvana t-shirt, and was exactly my type, but I was too nervous to speak to him. His name was Z, and he dated this girl named Claudia, with whom I had mutual friends. One time, I ran into them by the elevator between classes; Claudia introduced herself because it was still early in the school year, and we hadn't officially met yet. I won't say I had a crush, but I noticed him. There was a rumor that he slapped her in class one day; it was all anyone could talk about, but no one knew for sure. I would later ask him about this, and he said it wasn't true.

Four years after high school graduation, my depression was not improving. A couple of months prior, I almost died from diabetic ketoacidosis and was also dealing with living with my mother, whose mental health was becoming worrisome. Back then, everyone added everyone on Facebook. Even if you didn't know a person, you added them. There were about ninety of us in our graduating class of 2010, so everyone knew everyone, and we were all Facebook friends. Z and I must've added each other at some point, and that January, we started messaging each other. We both had trouble sleeping, so we would text or talk on the phone until early in the morning; we were falling for each other. He told me he had depression and anxiety, and I felt like that bonded us in a strange way. Two mentally ill twenty-two-year-olds with a ton of creative energy.

Though we were still just friends, Valentine's Day was coming up, and he asked me out on a date. We decided to meet at Tower City in downtown Cleveland. Growing up, Tower City was the spot to be downtown. You could shop, catch a movie, and hang out with friends in the food court. I was so nervous on the day of the date. We hadn't seen each other since high school, and I really liked him. I texted a friend and told her I hoped the date would end with a kiss; she told me to be patient and not rush things. I wasn't good at patience. I constantly worried that it would never happen if something didn't happen at that moment.

Z donated plasma that week and borrowed money from his friend so he could have bus fare and get me a small gift. As I waited in the food court for him, I thought about how badly I wanted him to want me. How badly I wanted this date to go well. When Z arrived, he flashed his friendly smile, and was wearing a black motorcycle jacket and distressed blue jeans. He looked different than he did in high school. He had facial hair and looked like a man. I realized I was in my twenties now too and no longer a teenager. I felt grown up, as silly as that may sound. He pulled a bag of chocolates out of his pocket. He knew I loved chocolate, and I thought it was sweet that he got me some. I was shy and quiet, and he was so cute. I asked if he wanted to go see what movies were playing; the theater was right next to the food court. I said I would pay for the movie since I knew he didn't have money or a job. I wasn't doing great financially either—I hadn't had a sponsored blog post in months—but I managed to save a bit from what I did make. He told me I should choose since I was paying for it. Halfway into the movie, I looked over to Z but couldn't read his face. I figured I could hold his hand, but I felt so awkward, and he looked uncomfortable, so I stopped, feeling embarrassed. I knew he liked me, or at least I thought he did. Once the movie ended, I told him I needed to buy juice because my glucose level was low. I was happy to have some distance between us, even if it was just for a few minutes. We left the theater and found a table in the food court. I noticed he looked uncomfortable as I drank my juice.

"Are you okay?" I asked.

"I'm feeling lightheaded," he replied.

"Here, have some of my juice," I offered.

He took a few sips and thanked me.

"Maybe it's because of the plasma you donated."

"Yeah, could be."

I needed to get out of Tower City; I felt embarrassed and couldn't breathe. We walked towards the library. Z walked ahead of me as we pushed through the busy mob of people. I rolled over the curb cut and felt my whole body going forward. My wheelchair was flipping over. I couldn't believe how awful this date was going as I lay in a puddle on the busy streets of downtown Cleveland. The weight of my wheelchair on my back didn't last long because a few men picked me up. I laughed it off so I wouldn't cry. Z looked worried and decided to push me the rest of the way to the library. At the library, we looked through books and mostly stayed quiet. I was ready to head back home. I headed to my bus stop, and Z hugged me. I didn't think he would text me later. I thought for sure that whatever chance I had with him was gone. I returned to my apartment and shared how everything went with my mom. She felt terrible about me falling but said she didn't think that would be a dealbreaker, and if it was, I wouldn't want to date him anyway. I texted my friend and told her everything that had happened; she told me it was the first date and that I should not be so hard on myself. I appreciated her efforts to make me feel better, but I was disappointed that he didn't kiss or seem interested in me.

I texted him.

"I feel like the date was awkward," I sent.

"You kind of made me feel uncomfortable," he replied.

I was shocked. How did I make him uncomfortable? What did I do? I replayed the whole day, and nothing jumped out to me. He sent another text.

"I could tell you wanted me to kiss you, but I haven't seen you since high school, Shalida."

My face burned; I made a fool out of myself. I was too forward, and I felt terrible for being so pushy. I apologized, and he said not to worry about it and that we should take things slow. We scheduled another date. I would go to his house this time, and he would show me around his neighborhood. Our first stop was a pet shop; the store was small, so I had trouble maneuvering my wheelchair around. He told me he would come here as a little kid to tease the birds, and the shop owners got so fed up that they banned him. In a playpen, there were about a dozen golden retriever puppies. He picked one up so I could have a better look. I started to get hungry, so he suggested we grab a pizza. We got to the pizzeria and split a pizza together.

Once we finished, we walked back to his house, which had stairs in the front. I was curious how he planned on getting me inside. I always get nervous when people pick me up, mainly because I fear being dropped. He picked up my chair with me still in it; I was amazed because I didn't think he was that strong. He told me his dad would have him and his brother help people move.

I was impressed. We got inside, and I met his youngest brother, who was homeschooled. He had an older sister who didn't live with them and another younger brother who I knew went to high school with us, but he said he had no idea where he was staying these days. His dad came out and introduced himself to me. He was huge with a bushy beard and rode motorcycles, but he was completely sweet to me. He told me not to feel uncomfortable about my wheelchair because he worked in a hospital as a phlebotomist and had seen it all. Z's mom passed away from brain cancer when Z was ten. When he and I first talked, he told me how cool she was and how she would play video games with him and his brothers and win. He told me he got into bed with her when she got sick and cried hysterically.

I now realize that Z and I were trauma bonding. Him from his past trauma and me from mine. That's why in the beginning, I felt so happy anytime we would talk or hang out. For me, he was a drug. I was extremely unwell mentally and unmedicated; I wasn't even in therapy. At the end of our second date, I waited for the bus to get home. He kissed me on top of my head, and every part of my body felt like a million butterflies.

Things were great in the beginning. Once on the phone with Z, I was so depressed about my diabetes and began to cry. I was genuinely just tired of being sick. For the past four years, diabetes had taken over my life. I felt like the universe had a sick sense of humor to give me a disease when I was already in a wheelchair. How much more could I take on? I remember bawling my eyes out on the phone with Z. He tried calming me down, but I was inconsolable. He told me to check my email. There was an email from him, a voice recording. He told me it was his cover of Pink Floyd's "Wish You Were Here." He told me he originally recorded it for his dad's birthday, but he figured it would cheer me up. It did. I stopped crying and listened to his voice. After that, I was in love with him and would've done anything to stay with him.

But then things started to change. One night we were talking on the phone, and I was telling him about my love of fashion. Suddenly his mood changed.

"What's the matter," I asked.

"This conversation is boring and unintelligent," he replied dryly.

My stomach sank and tears flooded my eyes. I headed straight to the bathroom so my family wouldn't see me cry. I texted my friend Morgy from college and told her what he had said. Morgy has always been a straightforward person, and that's why I still love her all these years later, even though we don't talk regularly.

"You need to dump him," she said simply.

I knew I couldn't, though. So instead, I told her I needed to think about it. I stayed in the bathroom, coming up with ideas for a conversation he would find interesting. I mentally came up with a list of my other interests. Would I tell him about my love of *Sailor Moon*? No, he would think I'm dumb. Maybe I could tell him about a favorite book? No, he wouldn't like it. Instead, I told him about my love of Rod Serling and *The Twilight Zone*. I grew up watching it, and it was my favorite. I washed my face to hide any evidence of crying. I texted him about how much I loved *The Twilight Zone*. He immediately replied.

"This is what I wanted, something interesting. I was thinking about breaking up with you," he said. That shook me to my core. I was so close to losing him that I made a mental note never to discuss fashion with him again. My stomach ached for the rest of the night while I listened to him talk about Dungeon and Dragons.

The third time I hung out at his place I was excited because we would be alone. At this point we still hadn't kissed. We sat on the couch when I got there, and he pulled out a necklace from his pocket. "I found this in the couch and wanted to give it to you," he said, smiling holding up the gold necklace. I looked at the necklace that was shaped like a Harry Potter Golden Snitch. I never really got into *Harry Potter*. I was happy that he gave me a gift, though. I thought it was sweet, and I put it on, posted a picture of it on my Instagram, captioned, "The sweetest gift from the sweetest man."

He picked out an anime for us to watch and twenty minutes into it he began kissing my neck, and we had our first kiss. It was passionate, and I could tell he wanted to go further. I was still inexperienced at that point, but I wanted to go to the next level with him. He pulled me onto his lap. "Let's go upstairs to my room," he whispered. He picked me up and carried me upstairs, leaving my wheelchair downstairs. Immediately he began taking my shirt off and then my bra. I was nervous but told myself I was ready to do whatever he wanted because I loved him. A couple of weeks prior he told me he watched a YouTube video by a disabled creator to learn about ways people with disabilities can have sex. I admired the effort he put into our relationship and my comfort. He asked for oral, and I gave it to him, because I wanted to. I loved him and wanted to show him in any way possible. He hadn't told me he loved me yet, but I knew it had to come soon. When we were done, we stayed in bed under the covers, listening to Mastodon and talking about what we wanted when we were older. When I got home, all I could think about was wishing I was still in his bed.

There were times we couldn't see each other because neither of us had bus fare. On these days, he would be short and dry with me. One day he was particularly antsy, and I was scrambling to figure out how I could make him feel better. In the back of my mind, I still had a fear that he would dump me if I didn't do something interesting or if he thought I was boring. I decided to write him a poem. This was a big deal to me because I hadn't been able to write poetry since I graduated high school, burnt out after four years of creative writing. I was anxious about writing a poem for him but decided to write a villanelle inspired by Sylvia Plath's "Mad Girl's Love Song." I titled the poem "Melancholy Lovers." I was excited to give him the poem, so I emailed it. Surprisingly he loved it. I felt great being able to change his mood.

At this point, I had only had the chance to meet his father and youngest brother. But one day, his older sister, Joy, was there when I came over. She seemed sweet; she was kind and asked me questions about myself. Z told me the two of them didn't have a close bond, so I didn't feel the need to impress her. However, I liked her. I hoped maybe we could become friends. We chatted for a bit while we waited for their father to leave. Even with us being in our early twenties, his dad did not want us to go upstairs. He had a rule that you had to be engaged to be alone upstairs, Joy told me as we chatted. But when his dad left, we went straight upstairs to Z's bed. A part of me felt a little guilty because his father was so lovely to me, but I physically just wanted to be with Z, and no rule would change that. We went upstairs, made out, then I put his shirt on and got under the covers. He grabbed my face and kissed me before saying, "No one can see your body but me." I nodded and kissed him back. It felt good to be wanted and adored.

I stayed for a couple of hours, and while we waited outside for my bus, I told him his sister was pretty. He looked at me and rolled his eyes, "She's not; she's so ugly." It wasn't like he was saying it as an annoying little brother, but like he meant it. When the bus arrived, I told him I wouldn't be able to see him next weekend because my mom, River, and I would be going to Pittsburgh to visit Point Park University since I recently got accepted. I didn't think to talk about our relationship and how it would work while I was going to be living in Pittsburgh. I felt like we were so serious at this point that there wasn't a need to have a conversation. He would visit me, and when I returned to Cleveland for the holidays, we would spend time together. It seemed like an easy enough plan.

On the bus to Pittsburgh, my mom kept bugging me, asking if I was still going to go to college or stay with Z. I told her I was going to school so many times, but she wouldn't drop it. After an uncomfortable Greyhound ride, we made it to Pittsburgh late at night. We waited in an area where cabs picked up people, but unfortunately, none came by. After almost having a breakdown because of how disorganized my mom had been on this trip, a car pulled up to us driven by a tall man with a thick Yinzer accent. He told us he was a jitney and could take us to where we needed to go for cheap. I sat in the front, and my mom and sibling were in the back. He drove us to our hotel, which was nowhere close to downtown Pittsburgh. He told us if we paid him extra, he would pick us up in the morning and drop us off. My sibling and I looked at each other, thinking that giving a strange man money ahead of time wasn't a brilliant idea. But my mom gave him cash and we headed inside to our hotel room. I hadn't talked to Z for a while, so I texted him letting him know I made it safely. He sent a thumbs-up emoji.

The following day, we got up early, and thankfully, the jitney driver was there outside waiting. Before I got into the car, he stopped me.

"Hey, did you pee in my car?" he asked.

I've always had a weak bladder because of my sacral agenesis. Leaks weren't that common, but I was mortified when they did happen. My doctors still hadn't found a solution for my leakage and wouldn't for a few more years.

All I could muster up was an "I'm so sorry."

He went on to say that he had driven the-R-slur people around before, so he was used to it, but he would need to get his seat re-upholstered, and he would have to charge my mom extra for that. My body cringed from hearing him say the R-word. It's so ableist and cruel. I looked to the backseat to see if my mother would say anything, but she didn't. She wasn't good at confrontation. All I could hope for was a smooth day at the college event. I was looking forward to going back to school and living away from home again. On the ride to the school, I texted Z hoping he could cheer me up. I didn't mention the leaking, but I did tell him I missed him. He sent another thumbs up. I was getting annoyed with his lack of communication. If we were going to be long-distance, he would have to get better at texting with me.

Once we got to the university, I relaxed, excited about starting school again. It was artsy and made me feel a lot more comfortable than the first college I attended. I thought about how Z would visit me and how we could get an apartment together. I knew he was once engaged to Claudia and the topic of marriage only came up once. He said he wasn't sure about us getting married because the engagement to Claudia scarred him. At times I wondered if he still loved her and at times it made me jealous. I wanted him to have those same strong feelings for me.

I decided to wait until I got home to worry about the situation with Z, but I went to bed that night with a weird sinking feeling in my stomach. We woke up around 5:30 in the morning to make it to the bus at 6:30. My mom told us that she had already paid the jitney driver the day before to pick us up to take us to the Greyhound. We waited in the lobby but once it reached 6:15, we knew he wasn't coming. I was livid. We were going to miss our bus, and my mom gave him the last bit of our money plus some to clean the seat. She called him, and he said he got drunk the night before and completely forgot. The receptionist at the hotel felt bad for us, so she called a taxi. We didn't have anymore cash but a bit more money on my mom's debit card. Once we got to the Greyhound station, my mom went straight to customer service to see if we could get on the next bus out to Cleveland without having to pay again. A wretched middle-aged man rolled his eyes at us and told us no. I've spent years trying to keep my mother's anger at bay so she wouldn't flip out on my sibling and me. Her frown showed me she was angry, and that River and I were easy targets. She called the jitney driver again to ask for our money back since he didn't keep his part of the deal. He said no, but for four hundred dollars, he could drive us back to Cleveland, plus extra because he needed to get that seat completely taken out and replaced. We knew he was lying. It made me angry that my mother just gave our money away without talking to us first.

Eventually, we got tickets bought for us by a family member in Cleveland. Unfortunately, they could only get two tickets for River and me. The last bit we had left on the debit card would have to go on a ticket for my mom. I was put in charge of purchasing the ticket online. Unfortunately, I put in the wrong time and got my mom a ticket for a different departure. She was furious and dragged me to the customer service office to fix my mistake. I felt so little and stupid; all I wanted was for Z to rescue me from that moment and from this life. The same wretched man told us there was nothing he could do. My mom didn't like this; she was standing over me screaming, "Look what you fucking did; you fucked everything up!" My mom never really hit us, but at that moment, I thought she was going to slap me. We went back to the lobby, and she wouldn't even look at me.

My phone needed to be charged, and the only outlet available was near the vending machine. I went and parked my wheelchair there, sobbing. I decided to call Z; I needed to hear his voice. It went straight to voicemail, so I left a message. "Hey, we haven't said this yet, but I love you and need you to know that." I was sobbing and hyperventilating, and everyone was watching me. I didn't care. Z called back, and he sounded concerned. I blurted out, "I'm sorry for saying I love you." He said, "No, I love you too." That was the first time we said those words to each other. For the next thirty minutes, he talked to me and helped me focus on my breathing so my anxiety attack would stop. He assured me everything would be okay, and he couldn't wait for me to return home. He even offered to send us money so we could eat lunch because I told him my mom yelled at me that her glucose was low, and she would pass out. I was happy to get on our bus and finally get back to Cleveland. I texted Z to let him know I was back, but he didn't respond. I figured there was nothing to worry about, especially since we told each other we loved each other earlier. My mom made it back later that night. She wouldn't talk or look at me. I was used to this behavior, so I knew she would return to normal in the morning or early afternoon.

After spending all our money on the trip to Pittsburgh, we were back to broke. Food was becoming low again which meant my anxiety was reaching a high. The previous fall I ended up in the ICU because of diabetic ketoacidosis. My mom told the doctors it was because I had food poisoning and couldn't keep my diabetic pills down. The truth was that we hadn't had any food in a week. I was vomiting up water. I was worried about getting that sick again, but mom didn't want to go to the food bank because she heard the neighbors whispering about her outside. River and I soon realized that there were no people outside. Mom was just hearing voices. Since we didn't have money for food, we didn't have money for bus fare, so I couldn't see Z. He was frustrated. To try to get him to relax I told him I would write him another poem. He was furious. "I can't kiss or hold a poem, Shalida. I don't want a poem," he complained. I apologized for suggesting it and tried to think of another idea.

Before I could think of anything, I saw that he was typing. My heart sank; he never took this long to type back to me. Once the message came through, I blinked, not realizing my eyes for already full of tears. "We need to break up" was the first sentence, and hot tears streamed down my face. My heart was racing, and I could only make out a few phrases "not attracted to you," "just the honeymoon stage," "Not important to me." I remember taking a deep breath and letting out a huge wail. The next thing I knew, I was in my mother's arms, sobbing, choking on my words. She rubbed my back and said, "I knew this would happen."

After crying for days, to make me feel better and to get my mind off him, River and I went to the library to get books. Rita Moreno had recently published her memoir. I loved *West Side Story* and thought Rita Moreno was the most beautiful old-Hollywood actress besides Dorothy Dandridge. She was also Puerto Rican and, me being half-Puerto Rican, made me proud of my heritage. I decided to fill my depression-soaked days reading, just as I did as a child. Throughout her memoir, I laughed and cried, finding solace in her humble beginnings and trouble with love. I felt hope when she told her story of meeting her husband, a doctor. I cringed at the stories about her and Marlon Brando. It felt too similar to what I dealt with from Z. This was the first time I acknowledged that Z was abusive. But Rita made it through it all. She found true love and had a baby girl. I read that book in three days, and by the third day, I knew that if Rita Moreno could get through everything, so could I. Maybe not that day, week, or month, but I would eventually get through it.

Even though I logically knew Z wasn't good for me, I still wanted him. I felt empty; he didn't give me a good enough reason why he dumped me, especially over text. I thought I meant more to him. During our relationship, I saw him as my protector—as a way out of my troubled life. I was hurt and angry that he let me down. I was hurt that he felt like it was so easy to hurt me. Days passed and I hadn't heard from him. Finally, just before my twenty-second birthday, I checked my email and saw a new message from him. My heart raced, and I braced for impact. I read the email quickly and sat silently, debating how to respond. I was pissed. In the email, he gave me his reasons for dumping me. He said it was because he cared more about hanging out with his friends than me. He said I was keeping him away from doing chores around the house. He said that we weren't a match. I cried silently, but this time it was because of anger.

I was a couple of months away from leaving for school, and a lot had changed besides the breakup. We were homeless, living with my grandmother in her one-bedroom apartment and with my aunt at her house. My mom began hearing voices. She thought the neighbors were reading her mind and hacking into her phone. The day we were supposed to move out because rent wasn't being paid, she called the police and told them the neighbors could see her text messages and were repeating them. The two cops looked at her, confused. River and I were embarrassed. They eventually offered to walk us to the bus stop because my mom was afraid the neighbors would follow us. I couldn't wait to get to Pittsburgh.

In the time leading up to school, I filled my days with talking to my future classmates and buying items for my dorm. Since we were homeless, I was able to use some of my SSI checks. Z still ignored my emails. I sent him an email telling him that I wouldn't let him, or any other man, treat me badly. Then, immediately, I sent him another email saying that I apologized for flipping out and that if he wanted, I could help him get groceries since I knew his family was losing their house. He told me to fuck off and to leave him alone.

College started off good for me. I was away from home, able to explore the city and join new clubs. But by sophomore year, my mental health was declining, and the stress made me start to miss Z. I was dealing with new roommates who made it a mission to make every day a living hell. I was suicidal, and would have breakdowns in my journalism classes. My favorite professor, the Pulitzer Prize-nominated Bill Moushey, was concerned about me. I can't count the number of times I sat in his office crying. He was the only supportive faculty member who noticed my downward spiral and tried to help, and because of that, I have nothing but the utmost respect and gratitude for his guidance and kindness.

In mid-December of 2015, I was on the phone with a friend before bed. We were talking about Z, and she told me it sounded like I missed him. I admitted that I did, and then I heard a beep from my phone saying I got an email. It was from Z. I was shocked and told my friend, saying I would talk to her tomorrow. I opened the email; it had only three words, "Can we talk?" I responded, "Absolutely." I wish I hadn't. I wish I would've made him feel ignored the way he made me feel. He responded with a long email telling me why he dumped me. He said he was thinking about cheating and wasn't in love with me. A woman at his job looked like Claudia, and he was looking up photos of Claudia to masturbate to when he came across one of my blog posts where I talked about

Claudia and how we had gotten close since Z dumped me; how we bonded. I had many emotions, hurt, anger, and confusion, but a huge part of me felt like the universe was sending him back to me because we were meant for each other. He said the blog posts hurt him because he didn't want me to communicate with her.

I was happy to hear that he read those posts, though; it made me feel like he might know how badly he hurt me. We caught up on each other's lives. He had moved in with a couple of friends. The next week was winter break, and I had already decided to drop out. My mental health was bad, and the school wasn't doing anything to help my terrible roommate situation. Z and I planned to spend the next weekend together; I would buy a Greyhound ticket and stay the night with him. A couple of days before I left for Cleveland, he called me to ask if I could make dinner for him. He wasn't religious but with it being so close to the holidays a good meal would be nice. Cooking has always been a way to show my love, so I agreed and asked him what he wanted. He wanted turkey, homemade mac and cheese, and cookies, but not just any cookies. They had to be butterscotch chocolate chip, just like his mom made. The mention of his mom tugged on my heartstrings, and I agreed on the condition that he would help me with everything. He agreed and then asked me, "Have you had sex with anyone since we've been together?"

"No, I haven't."

"Well, when you get here, we should have finally go all the way."

I hesitated because I was nervous about him hurting me again. Sensing my hesitation, he followed up with, "What better way to show our love than to finally make love?"

I agreed. In my mind, he wanted to get back together. Why else would he be planning such an eventful weekend?

Back in Cleveland, I got dropped off at his new house he shared with his roommates. I got there around seven o'clock on Saturday evening, planning to leave in the morning because he had work on Sunday. We would only have a night together, but

I told myself this would only be the start of new beginnings. Just as he had a year ago, he lifted me in my wheelchair up the stairs with no struggle. We headed into the kitchen and sat at the small table. Empty bottles of Jack Daniels littered the table, and I was curious to know if he had a new bottle. Jack Daniels had become my go-to choice of alcohol. He offered a beer that belonged to his roommates instead. I declined because I didn't really drink beer back then. Before I got there, I told him to preheat the oven for the turkey, just to heat it up. I cooked it at my granny's, so it wouldn't take long. The only things to make were the mac and cheese and cookies. I told him we would need flour, milk, and cheese for the mac and cheese. I was disappointed when he pulled out his sweetened vanilla almond milk. I made a mental note not to eat any. I knew I was too self-conscious and anxious to eat in front of him anyway, and after he finished eating we went to his room.

He sat on the edge of the bed and stared at me; I really took the opportunity to really look at him. I hadn't realized how tired his eyes looked. I was on the edge of bubbling over with anxiety; I was so hungry and regretted not eating anything, but I just wanted to watch anime and talk to him. A week prior we talked about exchanging gifts. I decided to make him a beaded bracelet in one of my LGBTQIA meetings. He recently told me he identified as demisexual, so I wanted to show my support, especially since I had just come out a year prior as bisexual.

I gave him the bracelet and he smiled and slipped it on.

"You remembered I told you," he said.

"Of course, it's a big deal, and I want you to feel celebrated for being yourself."

I also gave him a stuffy of the character Cake from the show *Adventure Time*. He told me it looked off-brand. The last gift was a rose quartz pendulum. He stood up, started searching through a box, and pulled out a Pikachu hat. He told me he got it in a subscription box a few months ago, and I could have it. I liked the hat because I liked Pikachu, but I was disappointed he didn't put effort into my gift.

Afterward, we got out of our clothes and into bed; at that point, nothing was sexual. We got under the blanket and pulled out my laptop to watch anime. We made it into two episodes before we both began touching each other. That turned into kissing, and then making out. He took off my bra and began to kiss my breasts. We did this for a while and started talking about why he reached out. I needed to know why he had reached out to me out of all his exes.

"Well, you're the only one who answered."

We started to make out again, and he gestured to his penis. I knew this meant he wanted oral, so I gave him some. When I was finished, I went in for a kiss because he had always kissed me after I finished. He refused, and I felt self-conscious.

"But you always kissed me after oral when we were together," I said.

"That's when we were together, the most I can give you now is gum."

He got up and tossed me a stick of gum from his jeans that were on the floor. Embarrassed and hurt, I chewed the gum and stuck it on his dresser. It was late, a little bit after midnight. I went to sleep but woke up around a couple hours later. I could feel him on top of me, fondling my breasts, biting them, kissing my neck, and pulling my hair. I was confused and groggy and asked what was wrong. I don't know why I asked him what was wrong but that was the first thing that came out. I asked the time, and he shrugged. I was tired and didn't want him to be doing this even though it was the same thing we had been doing earlier that night. I wanted him to stop but I didn't want him to get upset with me and risk losing him again. So, I let him keep going and I stared out the window at the Christmas lights outside at the neighbor's house. To me, they looked like red cherries glistening in the dark.

After he finished, he rolled over on his side. I went to cuddle, and he scooted further away. I went to sleep and when my alarm went off, I woke up, my face buried in his chest. He pushed me away and turned his back. I was annoyed with his hot and cold behavior, so I nudged his back and said in the driest voice possible, "My ride is coming; I need you to get me outside."

I wore the Pikachu hat to hide my bed hair, and we said an awkward goodbye. To this day I gaslight myself into wondering if what happened was assault. I waited a few days before I texted him. When I did, he was short and didn't seem to want to talk with me. The day David Bowie passed away, I texted to let him know, and he didn't respond. I eventually became restless and decided to ask him what his problem was. He gave a long answer about how he only wanted to be friends, but I wanted more. I texted him back, "You reached out to me, Z!" I was done with him and everyone else who had treated me like shit for the last year. That was the last time the two of us talked.

It took me a while to feel safe in a new relationship. I was always worried about what my partner really thought of me. When Cory and I started dating, I couldn't fall asleep at his place. He would stay up with me but eventually get tired and go to bed, but I physically couldn't get comfortable enough to fall asleep in bed with him. I talked to my therapist, and she said it's not unusual for that to happen, especially after what happened with Z the night I woke up with him on me. I finally decided to tell Cory why I really had trouble sleeping, and he understood completely. There has never been a moment where I've felt unsafe with Cory. Eventually, I would be able to fall asleep at his apartment with no problem. The first time I slept over, he held me until I woke up; I felt so safe and loved.

A few months after Cory and I got married I began thinking about Z and how he would tell me no one would ever love me. I found his Facebook and decided to message him to tell him he was wrong; someone did love me and thought I was intelligent and not boring. He blocked me. I was pissed; maybe it was petty of me to message him but blocking me was uncalled for, especially after all the shit he put me through. With the advice of my therapist, I decided to email him to let him know exactly how I felt because I had the right to express my pain. She made it a point to tell me that he probably wouldn't respond and that I would have to do this for myself. I told her this was for myself and sent this email to Z:

> I don't expect you to respond because I'm really doing this for me. You may not believe it, but you treated me like shit for years, made me feel worthless, and even told me no one would ever love me. Well, you were so wrong. Someone does love me—my husband. I want you to know that I've been able to move on and find true love—someone who finds me funny and intelligent (two things you said I wasn't). I came across your Facebook and wanted to tell you that. Blocking me is fine, but I needed you to hear this. This is for me to be able to have something I never had with you in our relationship, and that's a voice, because you always made me feel like I wasn't worthy of speaking. I truly hope you are well and have found whatever you were looking for all those years ago. I don't want to be friends; we don't need to be in each other's lives. I'm completely okay with that. I just needed to say my piece to help with my closure on that chapter.

When writing this book, I contemplated including this chapter. I knew our mutual friends would read it, and I worried about embarrassing myself, but this is a huge part of my story. My goal isn't to turn people against him, my goal is to heal. Writing has always been my therapy, and I won't let him or anyone else take that away from me. I still don't understand why it was so easy for him to hurt me. I told him about the book and asked one more time why he hurt me so badly, he didn't respond, and I know he won't ever. I'm one of those people who believe things happen for a reason. Being with Z wasn't easy, but I wouldn't be the person I am today without dealing with him. I can finally say that I have forgiven him. It wasn't easy, but it was important for my own mental health. I wanted him to be my protector from the abuse I was dealing with, I wanted him to take away my anxieties. Now I know that's not how life works. I hope he also finds love, even if it's self-love.

Melancholy Lovers

March 2014

I dreamed that you bewitched me into bed.
My body settles with the bottom of the wood.
A thousand suns going supernova.

Struggling through Lewis Carroll's land.
You must be dead.
I dreamed that you bewitched me into bed.

Licking the scarlet from my nails.
I must be dead.
A thousand suns going supernova.

The clock melts on the wall.
I wake up to pounding between my legs.
I dreamed that you bewitched me into bed.

Stretching, I form a bridge.
You drag me closer to your edge.
A thousand suns going supernova.

I must have gone mad.
We must be dead.

Little Black Girl Nostalgia

When I reminisce about being in a place that brought me pure joy, I think about when I was a little girl. A little Black disabled girl in her room coloring, playing with dolls, and reading old, tattered *Babysitter's Club* books. I think about being a tween skipping class in the bathroom with a group of girlfriends. Singing the latest hit from the radio, flipping through copies of *CosmoGirl* and *Teen Vogue* magazines, and reapplying an absurd amount of beauty supply store lip gloss. So thick and sticky but the only "makeup" we could wear.

Those are moments where I remember feeling free and happy. Black children are forced to grow up fast by society and our families. But being a Black girl brings a whole new layer—being treated like an adult, told not to cry anymore, and being sexualized by grown men. I loved dolls as a child and remember a moment when I was around ten or eleven and asked if I could get a doll for Christmas. I was immediately told "no" by my mother, who said I was too old for dolls and playing with any kind of doll would make me want to become a mother. Instead, I was given a Password Journal. A battery-operated journal that you opened by screaming your password into it. I loved that thing. It gave me an opportunity to improve my writing.

I don't fault my mother at all. She was doing what she thought made sense. She didn't want me even thinking about babies. She was a teen mom, having me at seventeen, and wanted to protect me the best way she knew how, though I do wish I was given the chance to be a child and play with baby dolls. The teen pregnancy anxiety went away as I got a bit older, and I think my disability played a huge role in that. I never left the house, and boys never showed an interest in me. I was doing great in school, so my mom got more comfortable with getting me things I was into, like Bratz dolls or stuffed animals when they could be afforded. I genuinely loved those things.

In the eighth grade, I used Toys-R-Us gift cards I collected to purchase a Bratz doll backpack. I wore it to school on the back of my wheelchair and immediately got disapproving looks from other girls in my class, who recently started wearing thongs and only carried their books in Victoria's Secret totes. I was in a weird place between wanting to embrace my likes but also wanting to fit in and not stand out as much as I already did as the "wheelchair girl." So, I started carrying a messenger bag. I also had a Bratz wallet that I carried until the beginning of ninth grade when a friend spotted it and told me to grow up. I threw it away and, for my birthday, was given a more adult-looking wallet by that same friend. A faux croc purple wallet with gold hardware. I loved that wallet and carried it throughout high school. But looking back now and seeing how kids on TikTok and Instagram are proud of their kawaii and anime merch, I wonder why I was so scared to wear what I wanted then. Even Bratz are making a huge comeback. Why wasn't I brave like the new generation?

It's strange but I think the adults around us, particularly the older Black women, didn't want us to be "fast" but also expected us to have a maturity level much higher than our white counterparts. Racism plays a huge role. Black children are immediately taught to survive the world. We have more dangers; we must act like little adults. It doesn't make sense to an outsider but it does to those in the Black community. By forcing us to act like adults, they mistakenly took away our childhood. Many of my friends who were the oldest child had to take on the role of a second mother, forced to take care of younger siblings. Helping with homework, doing hair, cooking dinner, and getting not only themselves ready for school but their siblings, too. This took away from experiencing a childhood of their own. I know some women now who say they will never have kids because they feel like they already raised their siblings. That isn't fair. Every child deserves a childhood. Even at a young age, Black girls are given the stereotype of the "strong Black woman." There's nothing wrong with being strong, but we are human and have human emotions. We cry when we're sad, we yell when we are passionate.

When I was in the seventh grade, I remember a teacher yelling at me because I asked her if she could discuss my grades with me in private instead of the busy hallway. I wasn't doing bad in my class, but I had questions I wanted to answer privately because I was a shy child. She began to yell at me because, in her mind, I was being disrespectful for even giving her a suggestion. I began to cry because that's how I reacted to yelling as a child. Soon I was pulled into a room by a group of older Black women teachers. They told me that crying made me look weak and that I had to be strong.

I got sent to the principal's office for the first time ever and got yelled at again by our Black male vice principal for crying and causing a scene that he said was disrespectful towards the original teacher who humiliated me. He had me alone in his small, cramped office glaring over me. I felt so vulnerable and afraid. As his voice boomed through the small space the tears kept coming hot and fast. When he was finished, he banged his fists on the desk and sent me out. I got back to class and cried until the school dismissal bell rang. At home, crying wasn't something that was really tolerated. I was labeled as overly sensitive or a crybaby. At the age of seven, I was told I was too old to cry.

The adultification of Black children is a huge issue. Black boys are seen as men by cops and the media. Black girls are not allowed to be treated as little girls in our society. We're taught that we must put our wants and needs on the back burner. We're told to be the backbone for the family, to hold everything together even though our tiny hands can't handle the burden of a larger, unjustified load.

This is why now, as an adult, I give in to the experiences I couldn't experience as a child. I'm telling the little Black girl inside me that it's okay to be who she is. So much was taken from me as a child—innocence, stability, and the overall feeling of safety. The anxiety I have now is the same anxiety I had as a little girl. I'm grateful for the Prozac and the therapy sessions because I truly believe they keep me going. I'm grateful to love the things I didn't want to stop loving as a child because society pressured me to grow up. Sailor Moon party? Why not? Stuffed animal collection? Definitely!

However, with healing the inner child, memories that were once pushed to the back of your mind resurface: like when I was fourteen, taking the bus home from an internship and an adult man kept flirting with me. I told him my age, and he said he had a daughter the same age. That didn't stop him from pestering me with inappropriate questions and telling me I "looked so grownup."

This was before you could scroll through your cell phone on the internet, so I just looked outside until I got to my stop. This isn't the only time I dealt with a situation like this. From a young age, Black girls are taught to be aware of their surroundings and to put their heads down in these situations. Given the violence so many women have dealt with by just saying no to any man, this is seen as a safety measure. But I can't help wondering how the world would be different if we taught little boys not to feel entitled to people and their bodies.

As I go about my journey of healing that little Black girl, I can't forget the teenage Shalida. During my teenage years, I was angry. I was angry about being poor, angry about being sick, and angry that my father refused to be in my life. In the ninth grade, I sat across from my mother at our dining room table sobbing because I realized my father wouldn't be there when I went to prom or graduated or received my acceptance letters from colleges. My mom sat there unmoved with a blank stare. She eventually shrugged and stood up and got started on dinner as I wiped my tears away. At the time, I was upset that she was so cold towards me, and I still am, but now I realize she was hurt that I was crying about a man who had refused to be in my life since I was a newborn, and she was the one who had raised me and made sacrifices.

My father met my mother when she was fifteen and he was twenty, and they were both working at a fast-food place. When they started dating, my father began abusing my teenage mother. She told me that when I was conceived, he forced himself on her. That fact still really fucks with my mind and affects how I view myself. When he found out that I was disabled, he decided to leave and marry another woman. He couldn't fathom that his child wasn't able-bodied or, in his mind, "perfect." He paid child support, but I never saw him until I was eight. I remember that day so vividly. I was so excited to meet my father and see how he looked. The next day at school was a "Donuts for Dad" event, where you could bring your dad to come eat donuts with you.

This was the first time the school was holding this event, and I was excited to show my friends that I did have a dad. I woke up early in the morning the day he was coming to visit and picked out my favorite blue raglan Old Navy t-shirt and jeans. We were staying with my grandparents because my mom and her husband had just separated. I was nervous. My granny helped me get ready in our room. She sprayed some of her perfume on me like she did with all the granddaughters before special occasions.

"Ready to meet your daddy?"

"Yup!" I nodded excitedly.

He was in the living room talking to my mom and sitting next to a woman I didn't know (I would later learn she was his lawyer). He looked at me and smiled and waved. I said, "hi." I was too nervous, so my mom did most of the talking. She knew I wanted to ask him about the donut event, so she asked on my behalf. He looked at me and said, "Of course, I'll come!" I finally spoke up and told him how excited I was about him coming. After he left, I started thinking about what I would wear to the event.

On the morning of the event, I asked my mom if she had heard from my father. He was supposed to confirm the night before because he would be taking me to school. She said that she hadn't been able to reach him. She looked sad as she put my hair into pigtails and took me to the school bus. Once I arrived at school, I wondered what I did wrong, why didn't my father want to spend time with me. Was it because I couldn't walk? Did he think I was ugly? Some of the kids at school started to call me ugly and make fun of my wheelchair so I started viewing how I looked at myself differently. As everyone else went to the event with their fathers, I stayed in the classroom with my teacher and other classmates who didn't have a dad. Suddenly, I heard a knock at our classroom door. I looked up, and through the window, I saw my grandpa (my mom's stepfather).

"Hey, Hot Rod, let's get some donuts!" he exclaimed, waving to me.

He skipped his morning shift to come and have donuts with me. As a little girl who had just been heartbroken by her father, I was disappointed that I had to have my grandpa take his place, but looking back at that moment, I am so grateful to have a grandfather who was there for me when my own father wasn't. I cherish that school event to this day, and I can't talk about it without tears of joy flowing. So maybe I didn't have a father who cared about me enough to spend an hour with me eating donuts, but I did have a grandpa who was willing to skip work so I wouldn't be disappointed.

It would have been amazing having a father during my teen years. But he made it clear that he could never be a father to me (his exact words, actually), and that my siblings, who he had with his wife, were his top priority. Looking back, I can confidently say that it's his loss. He missed out on having an incredible daughter because of his own idiocy. I'll probably never forgive him for how he treated me, and I know for a fact that I will never forgive him for taking advantage of my mother. I do blame much of my mother's mental health issues on what he did to her.

I'm not making excuses for her, but schizophrenia is a hard mental illness to have, and even though that doesn't excuse the way she treated me, I can look back and see how sick she was and still is. I've come so far into my therapy journey that I can hold her accountable without hating her. I can give her grace because by educating myself I now understand how hard it is to have a disease control your brain. She wasn't given a fair start in motherhood, like so many Black women. He was significantly older than her when she was a teenager; she was Black and poor. I sometimes wonder if, at seventeen, she felt like me being created was a way for me to save her. That maybe she felt like I was just an extension of herself rather than my own person. It wasn't fair that she had to raise a baby on her own while she was still a teenager, and the baby had a severe birth defect that called for so many hospitalizations and surgeries. The world didn't give her a fair start, and in this world, being Black rarely does; even though she's an adult now, the world has failed her so many more times. If I have learned anything as a Black woman in this world, it is that the world doesn't look out for us, and we must look out for each other. I will continue healing my inner little Black girl and teen because she deserves that. That's why I want to dedicate this chapter to my mother and all the Black women and girls society lets fall through the cracks; I'll try my best to make your stories bloom above the surface.

The Fashion Era

Late in the summer of 2022, *Dazed* online magazine reached out to interview me for a piece about disabled people's personal style and relationship to fashion. I was so excited because I was going to be featured on the website; it made me really dig deep to think about my relationship with fashion. I've modeled, been a personal stylist, and ran a fashion blog as a teen when blogging was still relatively new. I've dabbled in anything that would bring more fashion into my Midwestern life. When I was very young, my mom and I lived in a one-bedroom apartment. We shared a bed and shared a walk-in closet. This was before River was born, before my mom met River's father. It was just us two. I played with my cousins, but when they weren't around, I had to use my imagination. I played in our closet—slinging my mom's vintage Coach bags over my shoulders and trying on her clothes. Everything you could imagine a teen mom in the nineties would have: baggy jeans, oversized shirts, funky patterns, and a lot of gold jewelry. Everything swallowed my little body as I played dress-up. Even at a young age, I understood the fashion world. Flipping through *Jet*, *Ebony*, and *Vogue* awakened my inner fashionista. Seeing the top models of the decade, Naomi Campbell and Kate Moss, spread across the glossy pages developed my love of clothes and the art forms of design and modeling.

At one point, I wanted to be a designer but soon gave that up when I realized I could barely sketch stick people, let alone whole clothing lines. I figured modeling could be an option; I was still naive and didn't really understand that the world would be so judgmental of me. One of my favorite things as a little girl was going to the beauty salon. This rarely happened because we couldn't afford it, but when we could, I loved how the hairstylists would compliment me. It made me feel good to be told I was beautiful. On numerous occasions, older Black women who would be getting a roller set or relaxer would chime in and tell my mother, "Get that girl into modeling." I would sit there in awe that these women thought I was beautiful; this little girl in a pink wheelchair decorated with *The Lion King* stickers could model. Looking back, their compliments were probably half sincere, but they also wanted to make me feel good about myself. I was shy and didn't have much confidence. I stood out everywhere I went because of my wheelchair, so I tried to make myself as small as possible to avoid attracting others' attention. One day in the seventh grade, a former model came to talk to girls interested in modeling. I sat right in front as she talked about the glamorous life as a model in the eighties. She told us that we needed headshots so agencies would take us seriously. Afterward, she advertised her Mary Kay products she was selling. When I told her I wanted to model, the other girls around giggled. I ignored them. She told me she could see me doing commercial work, and I knew what I wanted to do for a career. I wanted to be a writer and a model.

She gave my mom and me a list of agencies to contact, and as soon as I got home, I started making phone calls. I was met with confusion when I told them I was disabled. "How can you model in a wheelchair?" Asked one agency. I was surprised that no one showed any interest. A model told me that I could at least do commercial work. The discouragement didn't last long. I used my copies of *Teen Vogue* and *Cosmo Girl* as study guides on how to have a model "look." I told myself that I would be the next big teen model star regardless of my disability. Around fourteen, I started seeing models like Jourdan Dunn, Karlie Kloss, Sessilee Lopez, and Chanel Iman all over my magazines. I figured my knowledge of fashion history would be something that would make me stand out. I was wrong. More agencies said "no" because of my wheelchair. I started to question if I was beautiful. I started to question my love for fashion. How could an industry I loved so much think my wheelchair was a dealbreaker?

Throughout high school I would spend hours in my room reading fashion magazines. When I was finished with them, I'd cut out my favorite pages and tape them all over my bedroom wall. In between the taped-up pages, I would stick Post-its around my room with words of encouragement, saying that I would be in those pages one day. With college approaching, I knew I needed to have an idea of what I wanted to do with my life, so I came up with being a fashion journalist. Whenever I told people this, they looked at me blankly like they were saying, "That's not a real job." I would then go into detail that people had to write articles in magazines, and it wasn't just photographs and perfume samples.

My best friend, Ace, was so supportive of me at the time. She always showed interest when I talked about the latest Dior runway show or gushed about owning a Chanel bag one day. We grew up similarly—in the inner city with single moms. We met on the day of our audition for the Cleveland School of the Arts for creative writing majors. We got stuck on the elevator together. Once high school started that fall, we instantly became close. She was truly like a sister to me; the kind of person to cheer you on the loudest. Even if I had the craziest ideas about getting into the fashion industry, she was right by my side, pushing me to do my best. In our junior year of high school, Teen Vogue came out with a handbook for different fashion careers. All the fashion-obsessed teens wanted it, and I was no exception. Unfortunately, we just couldn't afford it. I hoped that soon the library would get it in. I would spend my weekends at the downtown Cleveland Louis Stokes library branch checking out any book on fashion from their tiny selection. When I got home, I would lock myself in my room, absorbing the knowledge from design books or biographies about designers. Ace had just started working at a fast-food restaurant and was going to be getting her first paycheck soon. I hadn't mentioned the book to her, but one day before winter break, at lunch, she told me she had a surprise for me.

"I went to Barnes and Noble this weekend and saw this; this was made for you!" She exclaimed. It was the *Teen Vogue* handbook. I was shocked.

"Thank you!" I said.

"Of course! This way, you have some insider knowledge for when you become a fashion journalist," she said.

I studied that book religiously. Amid becoming homeless, the book sadly disappeared, but I am still so grateful for such a generous gift and such a great friend.

In my senior year of high school, I decided to start a fashion blog during my graphic design class. I named it The Fashion Wheel. I had just been diagnosed with type 2 diabetes and had severe depression. I clung to fashion as a way for me to cope with new life changes. I was inspired by Rumi Neely's blog, *Fashion Toast*, and her cool L.A. girl style. By that time, I was already into the boho fashion trend, and seeing Rumi in her beat-up Balenciaga bags and fringe skirts solidified my own personal style. I searched for other disabled fashion bloggers but couldn't find any. I was disappointed but saw it as an opportunity to make myself known. I started by posting items I had on my wish list. Then, I started sharing the outfits that I wore outside of school because we had a uniform. Soon, word spread around my small performing arts high school that I had a blog. People I never talked to before would stop me in the halls and discuss my latest post. For the first time, I felt like I was in the fashion industry. With my new confidence, I decided to give modeling another try, so I set out to submit myself to agencies. Still no luck, and this time, the agencies were even nastier with their comments about my wheelchair. I remember sending an email to an agency, and they sent me an email back that was meant to go to a coworker making fun of me.

Becoming a model wasn't happening, but my blog was jumping off. I made River my little photographer, and together, we came up with photo shoots and outfits. I would mimic Rumi Neely's outfits and try to recreate them with my thrift store finds. The hardest part about fashion blogging was that I didn't have money for clothes. My mom occasionally would give us fifty dollars each to shop at Forever 21, but other than that, we had to hold onto our clothes for years without getting them raggedy. As I picked up more followers and views, I started getting noticed by small brands who would send me their clothes for my review and photos. If there were small brands I wanted to work with, I would simply reach out and ask if they were interested in a collaboration. This got so much traction that I eventually was able to host giveaways for my readers. I started sharing more about my personal life. This helped set me apart from other bloggers because I was so open and honest about my depression and anxiety.

The first big, sponsored post I got was with Dove soap. I had to take photos and share something about my self-esteem. I don't remember the details that well, but I remember being so excited to get my first paycheck from a brand I loved and who wanted to work with me. It was only one hundred dollars, but that was so much to me back then. Nowadays, I would be called a "micro-influencer" because I didn't have a giant following, but brands still wanted my diversity. In 2012, with my blogging taking off, I decided to submit myself to the Ben Barry agency, a Canadian modeling agency representing mainly plus-size models. Ben was young and fresh in the industry, and he wanted to create a fashion world that had diversity. I took this as a sign that they would be open-minded about hiring a disabled model. I reached out to Ben Barry, sharing some photos and my story. Ben reached back to me personally, saying he loved my fashion experience and thought I was beautiful. He said he would check with his staff, but I didn't hear back from him again. I was heartbroken because I thought I had a chance. I soon learned that it probably had nothing to do with me and more to do with Ben stepping away from the agency. Currently, Ben works as a professor at a fashion college, which is fantastic, and it seems like he is still fighting for inclusion and equality in the fashion industry.

The next time I tried to get signed at an agency, it worked, and I got signed to the VisAble agency, which focuses on disabled models. I was excited to be signed, but no jobs were coming. My agent Louise didn't really know what to do with me, especially after I told her I couldn't go to a shoot I had finally booked in New York City because I just didn't have the money. She probably didn't think I was serious about modeling, which was far from the truth. That's when I decided to put more of my energy into my writing and to put modeling on the back burner. I had already been told "no" so many times and going after the big agencies like IMG and Ford seemed like a guaranteed no; I just couldn't hurt myself anymore.

In 2013, the Cleveland Goodwill organization reached out to me about creating a collection using items thrifted from Goodwill shops around the city. I was given two hundred and fifty dollars worth of vouchers to use. I had to choose my own models, but makeup and hair would be provided. I decided to go with a group of friends from high school and my younger cousin from my father's side, with whom I had just started trying to build a relationship. Coming up with a theme for the show was the easy part. I knew I wanted to pay homage to nineties grunge: Kate Moss, Marc Jacobs for Perry Ellis, and a ton of flannel. Looking back, my collection was terrible. It consisted of distressed denim shorts and ripped flannels, and I had the makeup artists apply a heavy smoky eye to each model. But at the time, I loved it.

On the day of the show at the Cleveland Aquarium, my father's sister texted me that my cousin couldn't make the show. I was heartbroken. Her excuse was that she needed to study. That would've been okay if I had backup models. After that, I blocked my father and anyone from his side of the family on social media. I had never asked any of them for anything in my life up to that point, and just like my father, they were letting me down. But even with the drama, I had fun, and I'm still so grateful for my friends coming through to support me and for Goodwill Cleveland for choosing me. During my speech where I talked about my collection, I broke down in tears thanking my friends for being my models. It was embarrassing crying in a room of over a hundred people but I'm a crier.

In college at Point Park University, a year later, I decided to join the fashion club. There was a small group of us, and our president would be leaving soon because she was having her first child. Somehow the position fell to me, and I took it as an honor. I could finally be surrounded by other people who loved fashion as much as me, but soon that dream began to crumble. Though being president of a campus club and being involved with numerous other clubs greatly improved my mental health, my friend at the time was the only one participating in the events I threw. There were twin sisters who came from a rich family who lived off campus, sporting their vintage Chanel and brand new 3.1 Phillip Lim accessories and clothes when they were on campus.

They had a massive following on Tumblr, and I thought it would be great for us to hang out since I also had a blog. Once, I invited them over to my place to show them the items I was donating to a women's shelter, and they were not impressed with my closet of thrifted finds and fast-fashion bargains. They ran out of there so fast. Whenever I saw them on campus, they wouldn't even make eye contact with me. I felt like such a loser.

My own blog started to transition more into a tell-all about my mental health and dating woes. I changed the name of my blog from *The Fashion Wheel* to *S.A. The Writer*. I started to fall out of love with fashion, mainly because I felt like there wasn't a place in the industry for me. Once my mental health began to get better and I was in a healthy relationship with Cory, my love for fashion started to return.

One thing in fashion I have always loved is bags. I loved designer bags even when I was a broke little kid watching runway shows on TV. The first bag I became obsessed with was the Burberry Warrior bag. At the time, I was in love with its slouchy design and studded surface. The second bag is a black Chanel medium 2.55 with gold hardware—caviar leather. That is my dream bag. Growing up, River teased me about wanting a bag that was so expensive. My mom would joke that I would have a closet full of Chanel bags one day. Because of the price tag, Cory breaks a sweat whenever I bring up someday owning one. It's still a dream and goal of mine to get one, even with the always-rising price tags.

By working, I have been able to buy a few bags that I dreamt of having as a kid. One year I bought a vintage Louis Vuitton Speedy 25 that was so beaten up that I got it for two hundred dollars. I sent it to the Louis Vuitton factory, and they were able to fix it for me. For my thirtieth birthday, I treated myself to a vintage cherry red Balenciaga Motorcycle bag. Yes, it's as beautiful as it sounds. Gifts like these give me a way to heal my inner child; also, it's a thrill finding a great bag that's just a bit beat up and needs some extra care. I love projects.

I won't lie—a part of me is disappointed in myself for not working in the fashion industry the way I planned. Life is so unpredictable that I know I'm not the only one who ended up doing something way off from their original plan. Sometimes I do wonder how my life would have turned out if I went to New York for college. I guess there's no point thinking so heavily about the past. Now, I work for a disability rights non-profit organization where I am a volunteer coordinator. It's a stable job, and I get to really help people, but it's not my passion. I always pictured myself as Carrie Bradshaw wearing fabulous clothes and storming the streets of New York. I started watching *Sex and the City* way too young!

I understand how some people may view my love of fashion as something that is materialistic or shallow. There are people in the industry who are that way (trust me, I know first-hand). They use fashion as a way to create a caste system. They view people as the haves and have nots. They don't see fashion as an art form but more of a way to gloat about their wealth. For me, fashion was always a comfort blanket. When I was going through my dark times as a kid, I used fashion to escape. It was the light at the end of the tunnel. I knew that if I made it through the dark times, I would have fashion waiting for me at the end of it all. I always told myself that I would get to a point in life where I could easily enjoy and celebrate my hard work by treating myself to fashion pieces I could only dream about when I was younger. I'm far from being rich, but I do cherish the ways I am able to give myself the things I couldn't have in my teens and twenties.

I took myself way too seriously with fashion growing up. Now that I'm in my thirties, I can really appreciate just having fun with it. I finally found my personal style. I'm more confident with wearing what I truly love and what makes me feel comfortable. Teenage Shalida would have never worn Tabi shoes because of the fear of being made fun of, but grown-up Shalida will rock whatever shoes make her happy. That took a lot of courage on my end. I used to be nervous about trying new styles, worried about how certain clothes would make me look in my wheelchair, like jeans and dresses. That's an experience many disabled people share. That's why I'm so stoked about seeing so many new clothing brands dedicated to making items that are adaptable for those with disabilities. Not too long ago, I sent photos to a modeling agency that specializes in disabled models. I haven't heard back, and I have a feeling that I won't. I'm at the age where, as much as I love the idea of modeling, I also love the idea of having a steady income and a safety net. I'm a Taurus, so stability means the world to me. The modeling world is rough, and I've gotten used to getting to bed by ten o'clock. My party days are behind me. I don't think I could if I tried.

There is still a part of me that holds out hope I can make some difference in the fashion industry though, because in a way, I'm still that little girl who woke up early on school mornings to watch Vivienne Westwood runway shows. I'm still the little girl who admires the craftsmanship of designer bags, even though a lot of them are still not within my reach. I'm not sure how, but I still have that dream. Besides, most great things in the fashion industry started off as a dream.

Taurus Energy

If I could paint the sky, I would scatter emeralds and lilies across it
Every night I would bathe in eucalyptus and sip on something bubbly
Time would be spent in the comfort of my zone
On summer days I'll dip my toes in the sage waters of the lake
while running my fingers through the grass
I won't shower the scent of Earth off my body
It will linger like Chanel
To rest, I'll lie my head on silk and cover my body in cashmere
Morning skies will saunter through my window, leaving rainbows on the walls
My coffee and toast will be made luxurious by just saying so
These will be the rules to follow as a bull

Vivienne

She's the woman who is eternally
ageless
a face that opens every door
lace lingerie
slung on the floor
cream silk
eyelash lace edges
a notebook
poetry and sketches
a designer bag
worn out leather
the way she likes it
it has a soul now she tells herself
a studio apartment with a cat
just like Tiffany she thinks
no that's not her name
oh yeah Golightly
Holly Golightly
she hated the book but loved the film
a gold lighter
stashed inside a pink Glossier bubble bag with her joints
for anxiety
or fun
black coffee in the morning
instant
no sugar
pasta for whatever meal she wants
vintage leopard coat
for the winter when it's so white out
her lips look even more like cherries in the snow

lovers for days
friends for nights
whiskey followed by a French 75
she's the woman who is eternally unforgettable
a vixen dressed in silk
a coquette in fur
a madonna in leather
she savors life
moving slowly like a water bead on a petal
pleasure takes focus
pain is temporary
life isn't forever
she's making the most out of this one she says
her black knee-high boots hit the pavement
onto her next adventure

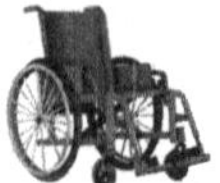

Drowning in Three Rivers

Content Warning: This chapter discusses suicidal ideation.

I can pinpoint a few moments in my life when I felt so depressed that I just didn't want to live. In 2015, I was a journalism major at Point Park University in Pittsburgh, Pennsylvania. That sophomore fall semester was tough. I lived with roommates who didn't acknowledge me and made moving into the apartment a nightmare, and the girl I shared a room with began torturing me mentally. She was a white girl from Ohio who used the N-word and kept her side of our room a mess. One day, she just randomly started ignoring me. Then, she would bring her friends over to make fun of me. Some of my clothes would come up missing, and she would put my cleaning supplies on high shelves.

My mom and River moved to a small town outside of Pittsburgh a few months before the semester began to be closer to me. Taking the bus to go home on the weekends was nice if I needed time to breathe and unwind from the pressure of school. But that didn't last long. In our small, cramped apartment, the neighbors started to harass us with racial slurs; after a grocery trip, my mom came back to the front door of the apartment broken open, and all our valuables gone. The police did nothing, and my mom's mental health declined. She became paranoid that the neighbors were following her around the city and leaving random graffiti messages. At the time, I was embarrassed, but looking back now, I understand she was responding to her personal space being invaded.

Also, around this time, I started talking to a guy I met on Tinder. He was a med school dropout who delivered food for a sandwich shop on his bike. Somehow, he always had a ton of cash on him. I never asked questions because I was so deep in my depression that I just didn't care. He was nice enough but somewhat of a snob, and he thought he was so much more intelligent than everyone else. But he was a good kisser, and with all the darkness I was feeling, I physically just needed someone to make me feel good. For our first date, we went to Nicholas Coffee and Tea in Pittsburgh. It was October, and the weather was crisp but not yet freezing. I wore a sweater as I sat waiting for him at a table outside. My friends sat at a table close by so they could make sure I was safe. He had long ginger hair that he constantly moved out of his face. He was cute and older than me and had an interest in me that made me feel kind of special. He asked if I wanted to go for a walk. I said sure, not thinking about how dangerous it was to leave my friends and go with him alone.

"Where are we going?" I asked.

"The north side, my neighborhood."

I had only been to the north side once and I knew it wasn't a short walk from downtown Pittsburgh. He rode his bike next to my wheelchair, and we headed to his neighborhood. On the way there, he told me he needed to stop at different gas stations. He said he had to masturbate a certain number of times in the day, so he would go into these gas station restrooms to take care of that. When he went in, I would sit outside, scrolling through my phone. Once we got to his neighborhood, we went to a sandwich place where we ate chicken tenders and fries until I started to get tired. I didn't get back to my apartment downtown until eight in the evening. We scheduled another date for the following weekend and texted throughout the week, not really talking about anything of interest.

For our second date, he picked me up in his Jeep. We went to a coffee shop. It was almost Halloween, so I ordered a latte that had a foam art skull on top.

"Wanna come back to my place?" he asked.

"Yeah, sure," I said.

"You know what, you're tiny but you have the biggest tits," he said smiling. We were still in the coffee shop, and I was embarrassed because an older couple was near us, but I just smiled. We got to his house, and he carried me inside first and then my wheelchair. I was taking a photography class that semester and needed some photos from a project. I pulled a camera from my bag and told him I wanted to take photos. I started taking still shots of random items in his place. A blue armchair and a lightbulb.

"Whatever, let's go to my room," he said.

His room consisted of a mattress on the floor and one dresser. I didn't really care because I grew up sleeping on just a mattress, and since I was in college it wasn't too unexpected. We got into bed, and he immediately started to undress me. Tossing my sweater across the room, undoing my bra as he admired my breasts. I was fine with it and was happy to feel anything other than the depression and anxiety I had been experiencing the last couple of months. I wasn't looking for anything serious, I just needed something to make me feel alive again. I needed to feel wanted physically. I was incredibly lonely.

"Holy shit, you're so fucking hot for a wheelchair chick," he said as he kissed my neck.

I knew it was a backhanded compliment, but for some reason, I couldn't muster up the courage for a comeback, so I let him continue to kiss me below my belly button.

"You're actually so hot," he said.

That wasn't the first time I'd heard that, so to me, it meant nothing. It was just another guy trying to "justify" that he was hooking up with someone in a wheelchair. I've often heard, "You're hot for a wheelchair girl." I feel like I've always hung between the sexualization of a Black woman and the pure ignorance of what people assume people with disabilities cannot do.

I didn't have sex with him, just a lot of touching and kissing. When we went to sleep, I woke up before him and listened to the rain hitting against his windows. I got up to see if he had any food to eat—nothing but boxes of instant ramen and oatmeal. I got back in bed, and when he woke up, he looked at me before laughing.

"What's funny?" I asked.

"What if I told you I had a camera in the corner of my room recording you letting me cum on you?"

My heart dropped for a moment. But at that point, I felt like I was already in hell, so I shrugged and told him to take me home. In my apartment, he got in my bed and was going to fall asleep for the second time that day. I started to run my bath water. He looked confused; I told him I had some work to do and that he should leave. After that, we never hung out again. Pittsburgh is small, so I would still see him in public, but I would look away from him. I don't know if he really recorded me that day. Sometimes, I randomly panic that there's maybe a video of me out there of me letting some guy cum on me and calling me his bad girl.

I was so close to just ending it all. I started sitting by the water at Point State Park. It's where the three rivers connect. It was November, and it was cold, but that didn't stop me from sitting there for hours wishing for a release. I tried the on-campus therapy, but it sucked and only made things worse. I knew I wasn't returning to school, and I couldn't trust anyone on campus, especially after a guy who worked in the campus radio station began making it hard for me to record my radio show. He was upset that I wouldn't give him a blow job. I told his professor, and the professor (a white male) replied by correcting my typos.

I felt defeated. I started making it a daily ritual to go to Point State Park. I would sit by the river and imagine letting myself roll into the water. Letting the water fill my lungs and take away my soul. Every day, I would get closer and closer to doing it. One day, after being called ugly by my roommate and her loser friends, it was too much for me to handle: the harassment, my mom's mental illness, and school made it nearly impossible for me to function. I was sleeping all day and only eating enough to be able to take my insulin. My mother saw me one day and began to cry because of how frail and exhausted I looked. I told her to stop crying because it wouldn't change the situation. I also didn't have the heart to tell her she was a large part of my brokenness.

The clouds were gray over downtown Pittsburgh, and whispers of rain were moving through the city. I went to Point State Park and decided that today would be the day. The rain would keep people away, so no one would be able to save me. As I sat there, I thought of every moment that got me to that point. No one was around, and the air was silent. The clouds rolled through the sky, and I felt a mist on my face. It was fall, and a sharp, brisk chill replaced any lingering warm temperatures from summer. The kind of chill my sweater couldn't fight off. Just when I thought I had the nerve to end it all there, I heard children laughing—two little girls with their father. I started to cry. I couldn't end my life now, not in front of children. I would be a reason for their trauma, and if I did that, I might ruin whatever future joy they had. I decided to turn around and go back to my apartment. On my way back, the sky opened and poured down on me. I was soaked by the time I made it into my apartment lobby. As soon as I reached my bed, I collapsed and slept until the rain stopped and the gray skies were replaced by dark night.

When I woke up, I lay in my bed and said to myself, "None of this is worth it." I was going to kill myself, and for what? By the time I made it to Pittsburgh, I had already survived so much. So much that should have killed me. I had to be tough. I was from Cleveland; I grew up in the Hough neighborhood, and I was a survivor. At that moment, I told myself I wouldn't let the roommate intimidate me any longer, I wouldn't give anything else to this university that refused to keep me safe, and I would go home, back to Cleveland. It was the end of the semester, and even with the chaos, I somehow managed to pass every single one of my classes with nothing lower than a B. I logged into my school account and withdrew from the university. I wasn't going to go back. School would always be an option, and I told myself I could go back anytime, but right now, I needed to focus on my mental health.

I let my close friends know that I would be leaving; some embraced me with love, and others called me weak and decided to go on the internet to trash me. But I knew what I needed to do. I've dealt with pain my whole life, and even in moments when it felt like it wouldn't go away, it always did. I always found a way to bounce back, and this time would be no different.

Once I moved back to Cleveland, I told myself that I needed to work on getting my mental health in order. Some nights, I would lie awake thinking about that day by the river and how those two little girls unknowingly saved my life. Other nights I had terrible nightmares where I did go into the river and was gasping for oxygen under the water. On those nights, I screamed out, "Mommy!" and my mom would come running into my room to check on me. I decided to start going to therapy and it helped a lot. I was almost angry with myself for not going to a real therapist sooner. At the college I was sent to "student therapists," who never gave me any real sense of hope.

For instance, I once told the so-called college therapist that my roommate was using the N-word. Her response was, "That sucks." But getting real therapy helped my mental health and made me feel so much safer around myself. I didn't feel like I needed to worry that I would harm myself. I started blogging again.

Drowning in Three Rivers: Part 2

After I left school, River and I would use the Wi-Fi at the Arby's up the street from us. I would go there to work on my blog posts and order a drink. After a while, one of the workers noticed me and River's routine and would give us free fries and drinks. Eventually, my blog gained the attention of a Latinx Influencer Organization that offers support to Latinx creators by connecting them to brands and offering workshops for becoming stronger content creators. I always knew about my Afro-Latina heritage because of my father, but until my early twenties, I hadn't tried to build a connection to that side of myself. I figured it was time to learn about my Puerto Rican culture, and fell in love with the side of me I once tried to ignore because it came from my father.

The organization saw my blog and invited me to a conference for influencers. They loved that I was bringing awareness to the disabled Afro-Latina community. They were holding the conference at Disney World. I was excited. When I was little, maybe four or five, I would regularly watch the same VHS tape about Disney World. After watching it, I would ask my mom if we could go. She would say, "Sure, let me call our travel agent." We didn't have a travel agent; we barely had food to eat. But now I was going to Disney World. The organization would pay for my flight and hotel stay at the resort. I wasn't sure if food was provided and knew that I didn't have money, so I bought a box of granola bars from the dollar store to take with me. I also didn't have money to check any luggage, so I somehow stuffed everything I needed into a purse. It was October of 2016, and it was starting to get chilly in Cleveland, but I told my mom to bring me a coat when I returned from the trip, so I didn't have to lug it around in Orlando. I was nervous because not only was this my first blogger event, but it was my first plane ride as well. I hadn't been able to pay my phone bill for months, so Granny let me take her phone to Florida because she didn't want me without one. I was all set to go, but my stomach dropped when a friend told me news about my ex-roommate from college. She was interning at Disney and was currently there.

When we were roommates, there were times she was violent by throwing things around in our room at the random guys she would bring over. Once, she was so upset a guy wanted to take her to a pizza cone place because she told him she loved pizza (she ate a large one every day because she was a picky eater). She didn't want a pizza cone; she wanted regular pizza. So she threw a tantrum, cussed the guy out, and began throwing her headphones and perfume bottles around the room. I didn't want to risk running into her. I didn't trust that she wouldn't try to make me feel like shit the way she had the year prior.

The day of my trip arrived, and I tried to stay calm so I wouldn't have an anxiety attack. I was nervous about the flight and experiencing turbulence. On the flight to Orlando, I sat next to a man who told me he was a native of Cleveland. He was a golf player and lived in Orlando but came back to Ohio to spend time with family. I told him about my trip and my blog, he was really impressed. During the flight, he talked to me to keep me from being anxious. At one point, he reached into his carry-on and pulled out several Malley's chocolate bars.

"I always bring these back to Orlando when I visit, have some." He said as he handed me a few. Malley's Chocolate is an iconic Cleveland brand. Growing up we didn't really eat them because sweets were for special occasions. But even I knew how delectable the pretzel crunch bars were. I thanked him and added them to my purse just in case I needed more food for the trip. We flew in silence for the rest of the trip, interrupted only by the pilot giving everyone Cleveland Guardians baseball game updates. The Cavs won the championship that summer and the whole city had our hopes up for the Guardians to win big that fall.

When we landed, we said our goodbyes, and he told me good luck with the conference. I was thankful for the kindness of the stranger. From the airport, I got onto the Disney Magic Bus that took me directly to the resort. From there, I was given my Magic band that would act as my room key and driven to my room by a cast member. I knew I would be sharing a room with two other women and was nervous, given my previous experience with bad roommates. I was the first to arrive, so I looked around and took in our huge room. The organization really went all out with our accommodations; I couldn't believe I was finally at Disney World.

Soon, my two roommates arrived, two Latinas excited to meet me and hear about my blog. One was a photographer, and the other was an entrepreneur named Hipatia who invented an empanada press to make it easier to close empanadas. It was already nearing midnight, and the three of us decided to get to sleep since our first meeting was early. As I tucked myself into bed, I decided to make the most out of this trip.

The next morning, we headed to one of the conference rooms, where we were served a Disney-themed breakfast. I leaned over to Hipatia and asked, "Do we get free food here?"

She laughed, "Of course, they provide all of our meals and even some of our alcohol." I was happy that I wouldn't have to survive off chocolate and granola bars for the week. As I looked around the room, I got overwhelmed with the amount of people. I've always been shy around new people so I knew this would be a lot for me to handle. A server came over to me and asked if he could get me anything. I was so overwhelmed by the amount of food it must have been written all over my face because he asked, "How about a little bit of everything?" I nodded and whispered, "Thanks." Soon, a pile of pastries, fruit, coffee, tea, and the most decadent hot chocolate was in front of me. I smeared jam from mini jars of Bonne Maman onto a piece of toast and ate it as I people watched. I recognized parent bloggers and famous Instagram creators; I recognized Chef Ronaldo Linares from The Food Network show, *Chopped.* He is also one of the top Latino chefs in the country. I was having a moment where I needed to pinch myself because I couldn't believe I was invited to such an important event. It felt like my hard work was finally paying off.

We spent the first hour introducing ourselves and doing some networking. Afterwards we were invited to a yoga class. We walked into a room that had a table of more food and on the floor were rows of pink yoga mats. I got out of my wheelchair and got down on a mat. I took a few yoga classes in college and was happy to have the opportunity to work out. One thing I appreciated was that no one told me how inspiring I was or made a big deal out of me doing yoga as a wheelchair user. It made me feel normal for once in my life. After yoga I grabbed some snacks and a water bottle and sat at a table of older women. When I came over, they were speaking Spanish, and I couldn't really understand much.

Seeing the look on my face one woman switched to English, "she doesn't speak Spanish, ladies." Soon the women all nodded and introduced themselves in English, except one woman with a gray bob haircut named Wanda. She lived in Puerto Rico and took care of her disabled son who was also in a wheelchair due to cerebral palsy. She didn't know much English and I didn't know much Spanish but somehow we were able to have a meaningful conversation and really form a bond. Another woman I met at the table was Christine, who ran a successful parenting blog where she talked about how her and her husband raised their son with autism. I felt like I found my people. I felt safe with these older women and looked up to them as abuelitas y tias.

A guy came up to me at the next seminar and introduced himself; his name was JP Dominguez and I thought he was most dreamy looking guy. Thick black hair, the cutest smile, brown eyes and tan skin. He told me he was studying law at Pepperdine University. His mother was a lawyer and a very well-known one. He told me his brother was hard of hearing and was an ASL interpreter. He wanted to introduce himself because he thought my disability rights advocacy was cool. I also learned that his family owned their own media production company that supported Latinx creators. I can't remember how long we talked, but by the end of the conversation, I felt like I had known him my whole life. While we talked, a videographer asked if we wanted to be interviewed for a project about discrimination. We went into a room that had a green screen. The man (who never told us his name or who he worked for) told us he wanted us to talk about a time we dealt with adversity. We both looked at each other, almost like we were telepathically saying, "This should be easy." I decided to go first because I learned that if I do something that makes me anxious before anyone else, I can get it out of the way and be done with it. I talked about when I signed up for the girls' tennis team in high school, but was pulled into the coach's office.

"Shalida, how can someone in a wheelchair play tennis? How will you hit the ball?"

I was shocked and hurt. I thought everyone knew that people in wheelchairs could play tennis. Growing up, I was involved in a few sports: soccer, basketball, and ballet. All of which were for disabled children. I loved every single sport I was in and wanted to try tennis so I could also have more extracurricular activities for my college resume. As a teen, I didn't know how to advocate for myself. So, I just sat there and mumbled. "I don't know." I don't know why this incident popped into my head but it did, and I went with it. I sat in front of the green screen, and once the camera started shooting, I poured out the story, and eventually began to cry. Once I finished, the director thanked me for being so vulnerable. JP hugged me, and he went up next. He talked about his mom being an immigrant and becoming a lawyer to help other immigrants. The director told us we would hear from him soon, but we ended up never hearing from him. A couple of years later, JP and I laughed about how we let this random man put us into a room to film us.

After the interview, I started feeling sick, so I decided to rest in my room. I could feel a fever coming on and just wanted to sleep. Once I got back to the room, I took a bath and slept until it was time for the cocktail party. When I woke up, I threw on a bit of makeup and put on a black long sleeve bodysuit with a black maxi skirt and made my way through the resort to the cocktail party. I found the women I had met earlier and sat with them at a table. The music was blasting, and workers were passing out drink tickets we could take to the bar for free drinks. On the side was a table full of food. I put a few items on my plate because I still wasn't feeling great. I headed up to the bar, nervous because I didn't know what I wanted and didn't know much about cocktails. I ended up ordering a margarita. Once I was back at the table with the abuelitas y tias they started asking me about my Latina side. I told them about my father, and they said he should be ashamed of being such a deadbeat. A lot of the women were from Puerto Rico and wanted to know which part my father's family was from, and I told them San Juan. I didn't know much about that side of my family but that was one piece of information I had.

Before long, everyone was dancing and drinking and yelling Wepa! I asked what it meant and was told that it meant joy. I started yelling it, too. As the party was winding down, me and my roommates headed back to our room to catch the last parts of the Hillary Clinton and Donald Trump debate. I went to bed thinking that my life had fully turned around. I was on my first brand trip at Disney World, and Hillary was definitely going to be president. When I woke up in the morning, my fever was back, and my body ached. Hipatia tapped me and asked if I was coming for café y jugo. "I don't feel so well," I squeaked from under my blanket. She put her hand to my forehead. "You're burning up!" she exclaimed. I reached for the nightstand next to my bed and grabbed another pain reliever. "How about you just rest, and I'll get you for lunch?" I nodded and went back to sleep. I ended up waking up not too long after Hipatia and my other roommate left. I threw on some clothes and headed to breakfast. When I got there, I found an empty table, and as soon as I sat down, a waiter brought me a plate of Mickey Mouse waffles poured some orange juice. I knew I needed to eat even if I didn't feel well.

"Oh good, you must be feeling better!" Hipatia shouted across the room.

My fever wasn't as bad, so I nodded. Once I finished eating, I was able to go around to the different rooms where seminars were being held. The first seminar was for a VR game set. I saw JP there, and my heart fluttered a bit; I only hoped I didn't look as sick as I felt. Once he spotted me, he came over, and we talked for a bit before trying on the VR headset. Seeing how accomplished JP and everyone else was at this event made me want to push myself even harder to be a better content creator.

Later that night was a big awards ceremony, and even though I knew I wouldn't win anything, I still felt excited just to be able to go. When I returned to my room, I curled my hair and put it in a loose updo. I put on red lipstick and wore a black maxi skirt from the night before with a black and white striped halter top. I decided to vlog a bit for my YouTube channel before heading to the ceremony. As I headed to the ceremony, I could feel the fever creeping back, so I popped another pain reliever and prayed I would be able to make it through the night. The humidity from the Orlando weather, coupled with my fever, wiped me out but I wasn't going to let anything stop me from fully enjoying this opportunity.

Before I got to the ceremony there was a red carpet with a step and repeat banner displaying logos from all the sponsor brands. I met up with Ronaldo and Hipatia and we took selfies and got solo shots of ourselves. Then we headed to the ceremony. We all decided to sit together at the same table. Waiters came around with our meals for the evening and poured wine and champagne. I had no appetite but managed to get a bit of fish and pearl couscous down. When I told the waiter I was finished, he looked concerned that I really hadn't eaten. He asked if the chef could make me something else. I told him no that the food was fine. I was just looking forward to dessert, which was Mickey Mouse chocolate mousse cakes. I had no problem getting the chocolate treat down. Soon, they began handing out awards. Excitement was felt throughout the room; people hugging and cheering for friends and family. I was happy, too, and the painkillers from earlier had already lowered my fever. Later, everyone was on the dance floor. I danced that whole night. Spinning around from Ronaldo to JP and to anyone else who wanted to dance. For the first time in a while, I felt happy to be alive. I slept well that night. The only sadness I felt was about leaving this magical place.

I woke up with no fever and an urgency to make the most out of the last day of the trip. I lingered around the resort and took in the humid air and palm trees because I knew I would soon be back in frigid Ohio. I went to almost every seminar that was available and made sure to enjoy the endless supply of food. That night we would be having a pajama party to celebrate the last night. I only brought my ratty old Pink Floyd shirt to sleep in, but I didn't care. I was just happy to spend one last night with my new familia. Later, we were told that Disney wanted to gift us each a ticket for the park to use that night. Unfortunately, it was during the same time as the pajama party. I wanted to explore the park and finally see Disney World, but I remembered my racist ex-roommate worked there. Logically, I knew it was improbable for me to run into her, but even the thought of a slight chance sent me into a panic attack. I decided to enjoy the pajama party and skip the free ticket to the park.

The pajama party was nice; we were served a variety of sweets alongside a chocolate fountain. Before I knew it, midnight was approaching, and my flight was early in the morning, so I decided to say my goodbyes and get to bed. Before I left, the abuelitas y tias told me to work on my Spanish. I agreed and hugged each last one of them. I got up super early to take the Disney shuttle to the airport so I wouldn't be late. I managed to stuff my purse with most of my freebies, and I slung my new bright pink yoga mat on the bag of my chair in hopes that TSA wouldn't make me check it.

Once I got to the airport, I could feel my fever coming back but I already went through my supply of pain relief pills. I decided to put on a brave face, and once I got home, I would be able to rest and sleep off whatever this was. I wish the return flight went as smoothly as my flight coming into Orlando, but I was on a budget airline cramped in a tiny seat between two kids and their parents behind me yelling about how they wanted the whole row for their family. Once we took off, I began to have a full-blown panic attack. I closed my eyes as tight as possible. The fever was kicking my ass, and the anxiety attack was heightening it. I just wanted to get home to Mom and River. Once we landed and everyone got off the plane, I felt like I could breathe. It took me a moment to find my mom in the crowd of people, but soon, she spotted me and ran over with my winter coat. It was fifty degrees in Cleveland, and my body was in shock from the huge difference from the sunny Orlando weather. She hugged me and started to cry when she felt my forehead. "You're burning up!" she cried. She pushed me, and we went on our bus route to get home.

When I got home, I immediately started editing my vlog and made a note to go to Arby's the next day to upload it. A few days passed, and my period came, and the fevers I was experiencing stopped until the next month when it would happen all over again. I started doing research and learned that other people had experienced fevers before their menstrual cycles. For a few days before my period, I would be stuck in bed with low-grade fevers, and they wouldn't stop until my period came. I added this to the ever-growing number of health issues the universe cursed me with. I began working on a couple of short stories, and since I was stuck in bed a lot of the time, my depression began to get bad again.

Things really got bad when we found out we were getting evicted. There wasn't a real reason as to why we were being evicted other than the apartment complex manager, Candy, was a huge bitch. All the tenants disliked her. Mainly because one time someone working in the office stole everyone's rent, and Candy made everyone repay the amount. This left a lot of people, including my mom, behind on bills and rent. She also had something against me. Sometimes if I needed to print something the receptionist would let me use the printer, but anytime Candy would see me in the office, she would make it a point to roll her eyes at me and go into her office and slam the door. Soon, we were going to stay with Granny. We were with her for a few days before an argument with mom happened, and she wanted us out. It was a snowstorm, and the three of us, me, Mom and River, were sitting outside in the snow, waiting for a cab to take us to my mom's brother's place. As I sat there feeling the tears freeze on my face, all I could think about was how I was having the time of my life only a couple of months ago. Christmas was in a couple of days, and I was homeless and depressed, and a small part of me wished I had just drowned in the three rivers in Pittsburgh. I didn't know how much more the world thought I could handle.

Sensitive

It's not the end of the world
if you don't bring peace to the world
You don't have to cry
You don't have to fear
The way of the world
This job is too big for one person
Take it easy
Take a breath
You're not to blame
For how the world fails
You can keep shining
You can breathe out
You're only human
You bleed like everyone else
Feel all your emotions
Don't let them bubble over
But don't let them halt your journey
Don't crumble

Prozac Saved My Life

I was born with the initials S.A.D. I don't think anyone really noticed it. I always found it fitting, since I have always been sad. When I was seven, a boy who rode on the school bus with me asked if we could play together. He was also in a wheelchair and got teased a lot, so I told him no, mainly to save myself from any more bullying. A teacher's assistant at the school told me I should play with him. Every day, she would ask if I played with him, and every day, I told her no. Before winter break, both second-grade classes came together for a winter holiday party. I saw him across the room alone with no one beside him. I decided I would play with him after the break, but at that moment, I wanted to watch Pokémon and slurp Gogurts with my friends.

The day we got back from break the mood at school seemed somber. I noticed the boy hadn't been on the bus. The teachers gathered everyone to let us know that the reason the boy wasn't in school was because he died from his cancer. No one knew he had cancer. We all just assumed his wheelchair was because he was disabled, like a lot of us at the school. We each took home a letter explaining the situation and letting our parents know counseling would be available. That night, my mom and stepdad were making spaghetti (my favorite), but I turned it away. I wasn't hungry.

"Why aren't you eating?" My mother asked.

"My stomach hurts," I said quietly.

Both she and my stepdad looked at each other with raised brows.

"Let's play hangman," my stepdad announced.

I loved playing hangman because I love anything dealing with words. I almost always won. I decided to go first, and I went for a six-letter word. Quickly, they figured it out: Cancer.

"Why did you choose that word?" My mother asked.

"I don't know," I said, excusing myself from the table and going to my room.

Over the next few days, my stomach pain became worse, so my mom let me stay home from school for a day. In my mind, I knew exactly what was wrong with me. I thought I had cancer, too, and I got it because I wouldn't play with the boy. This was my punishment. I didn't have cancer, but I was completely convinced that I was going to die any day. At school, I found it hard to concentrate on work because I was consumed with when or if cancer would kill me. At home, I started saying my prayers before bed every night, making sure to name every person in my life.

In fourth grade, we read *Sadako and the Thousand Paper Cranes* by Eleanor Coerr. The teacher read the story about a young Japanese girl who was dying from leukemia after the atomic bombing of Hiroshima. I raised my hand and told the teacher I couldn't breathe. She came over, and I instantly cried. Not a silent weep but a cry so loud the class next door could hear me. The teacher's assistant escorted me to the bathroom, where she held me and wiped away my tears. She asked what was going on. I told her that I was afraid that I would die just like the girl in the story and just like the boy from second grade. She reassured me that everything would be okay and that I was fine. I didn't believe her. After this incident, the school called child protective services on my mother, and I got in trouble for crying in school and bringing attention to our household. After that, going forward in school, I always reminded myself never to talk to teachers and never to cry in front of them.

When I was ten, I developed a fear of choking, so I only ate liquid foods and would spit out my dinner in the trash. It's something I'm still not completely comfortable talking about, but I hope one day that will change. If anyone takes anything from this book, please know that mental illnesses can happen to anyone, and it doesn't make you a weak person. I got called weak a lot growing up because I couldn't handle my food insecurity or homelessness; the truth is that I shouldn't have had to go through those things. There's a huge emphasis on taking care of your physical health, which is important, but often mental health is forgotten about. My fear of choking went on for so long that I lost a lot of weight, and I freaked my mom out. My pediatrician told her just to give me milkshakes, and I would gain the weight back. My anxiety soon developed into severe OCD and depression. In high school, I was convinced I had contracted Lyme disease even though I had no contact with any ticks. It wasn't until my mid-twenties that I knew that I needed to be medicated. I started therapy, and it worked well enough, but I was still clearly mentally unstable. I needed drugs to help my brain.

When I was a preteen, I watched Christina Ricci portray Elizabeth Wurtzel in *Prozac Nation*, the film adaptation of Wurtzel's nineties memoir. This led me to dive deeper into Wurtzel's life. I think even then, as a preteen, I knew that one day I would need medication. Other girls my age didn't act the way I did; some were nervous, but rarely did I meet others who shared my sense of doom and fear. I knew I needed to take control over my life. I didn't want to look out for even numbers or touch certain areas in the kitchen to make sure a loved one wouldn't die. I scheduled an appointment with a psychiatrist, and she told me that the best option for me would be Prozac. I was excited. For once in my life, I felt like maybe I could live a "normal life," whatever that meant. I started on the lowest dosage, and since then, I have increased as needed. I still have OCD, anxiety, and depression, but everything is so much more manageable. I don't feel like I'm drowning. Everything doesn't work the same way for everyone so I can only speak for myself when I say that I have seen a huge improvement in my mental health because of the tiny capsules.

Occasionally, when I'm swallowing my morning pills (carefully because the choking fear is still there), I think about how Carrie Fisher had a giant porcelain Prozac pill in her house, and when she passed away, her ashes were put into it. How cool is that? I don't know if that's what I want done once I die, but I do want my own giant Prozac sculpture. I'm not trying to sell you Prozac, and I promise I don't work for Big Pharma. I just think it's important as a Black woman, who shares so much about my life, that I should also share how I deal with my mental health. Mental health care is such a taboo in the Black community. Many Black elders have lived through much trauma without any therapy. Getting medicated for mental illnesses is even more frowned upon.

When I started taking medication, so many people close to me would tell me how sorry they were for me. "That's terrible," they would say with the most pitiful look. I never understood that because I was so much healthier. "Don't be sorry, it saved my life!" I would exclaim. And that wasn't me being extra or anything. I truly feel like it saved my life. I'm not perfectly mentally healthy, and I still have my struggles, but I can honestly say that being medicated has made me get through those times a bit easier.

I hope that if you are going through some mental health crisis, you feel confident and supported enough to get the help you need, no matter how that may look. I don't know if I will always be on Prozac, but I do think I will always need some sort of medication and I'm okay with that. Self-care isn't always glamorous; sometimes, it's just putting your pills into an organizer for the week.

Flawed

I fell down a thorn covered hill
My skin dotted with blood
My hair tangled in vines
I reached for you
I looked for you
Tears stained my cheeks
Leaving white tracks like an avalanche
I called out to you
I wasn't smiling so you never came
I had no laughter so you ignored my cries of your name
You only like it when my skin is dotted with peace
You only like it when my hair is untroubled
You only like it when my cheeks are flushed
You only answer to a smile
I wish you loved the flawed parts of me

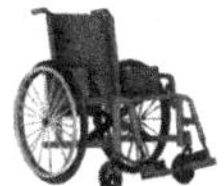

Daydreaming Feels So Good

I used to think my constant daydreaming was a sign of my creativity but it was, in actuality, a sign of my mental illness. I learned about maladaptive daydreaming a few years ago. It's a coping mechanism that can show up particularly in those who suffered from childhood trauma—which I experienced a lot of. When I was kid, I would daydream from day to night. Coming up with scenarios that always put me in situations where I was famous and rich. I was beloved and had a stable life, a cozy home, and plenty of food. This makes sense to me now as an adult because as a kid those were things I didn't have all the time. As I have gotten older, I've realized that my maladaptive daydreaming is the least annoying symptom of my mental health issues. For me, it's harmless, and I don't find it getting in the way of work. It's a coping mechanism, but I don't view it as an unhealthy one. I also don't do it as much as I have gotten better mental health care; and I've learned more efficient coping mechanisms, like listening to music and getting back into journaling.

The difference between regular daydreaming and maladaptive daydreaming is that you do it constantly. It's an obsession that distracts you from everyday life activities. I don't remember much of the third grade, but I do remember the daydreams I had. Around that time, my favorite daydream was about me being a Pokémon trainer and traveling with my Togepi. I was so absorbed in these daydreams that I never participated in class. I'm not sure how but I managed not to fail. School always came easy for me, and I was a fast learner. The only subject I struggled with was mathematics, and that was because of my undiagnosed dyscalculia.

When I was in the third grade, my mom and stepfather had just separated after a tumultuous marriage because of my stepfather's infidelity and abuse. This made my mom severely depressed and very short with me and my, in her words, "weird phases." I was at a new school and had trouble making friends. River was a toddler, so I spent most of my time in my room watching Olsen twin movies and, of course, daydreaming. At summer camp that year, I met a girl who was also in a wheelchair who was a couple of years older than me. I learned that she was also a daydreamer, and we spent the whole week sharing our daydreams and coming up with stories. When we got picked up by our families on the last day, I scribbled her information on a piece of paper so we could stay in touch. Unfortunately, that never happened because I used one of the highlighter gel pens I begged my mom for, so I couldn't even see her phone number on the white paper.

My daydreaming didn't stop as I got older. As a teenager, I would daydream about finding love and having a stable home life. I can't remember where, but I remember hearing that daydreaming is a form of manifestation. I can see how that would work—if I really look at my life, I believe that I manifested some things. For so long, I daydreamed about having a healthy and safe romantic relationship, and one day, I decided to go on a dating site, and that's how I met Cory. I wasn't even actively looking for anyone during that time.

After moving out of a homeless shelter, I took the opportunity as a sign that my daydreaming (or manifestations) were paying off. When Cory and I first met after texting for a couple of weeks (for hours at a time), it was December 30, 2017, and we decided to meet at a coffee shop in Geauga County, where I lived with my mom and River after leaving the shelter. It was practically a blizzard, but Cory still drove the distance to come and meet me. I got there before him, found a table in the corner of the shop, and ordered a hot chocolate to warm me up. He showed up a bit after, and I was immediately smitten. We shared chocolate truffles and talked for a couple of hours. I didn't want to say goodbye, so I suggested our next date could be at his place. I think we both knew after that first meeting that we would always be together. We had an immediate emotional and physical connection. Every weekend he would pick me up, and I'd spend the weekend with him at his apartment. He would take me out to new restaurants and plan romantic dates and vacations. A couple of months into dating, I was sad because I got rejected from a writing gig in California, and he held my hand and told me not to worry, that he would take me to California, that he would take care of me. After six months of dating, we knew we wanted to see each other all the time, so he spent his inheritance from his grandfather to buy us a wheelchair accessible house in the suburbs. For the first time in my life, I felt like I had the stability and unconditional romantic love that I would always daydream about. Even now, we tell each other we are each other's soulmates, and I really do believe that. It truly feels like I manifested meeting him. So, I'll take that as a win for my daydreaming.

Another thing I find myself daydreaming about often is being a mother. I always wanted to be a mom, and I can remember having these daydreams at a young age. I didn't start thinking about my own fertility until I met Cory. I learned early on that because of my sacral agenesis, pregnancy could cause some severe complications. The main complication is that the doctors don't know what those complications could be. Sacral agenesis is so rare that there are no records of a successful pregnancy—or at least that's what the fertility specialist at the Cleveland Clinic told me. As soon as I met Cory, I knew I wanted to spend every moment with him. I wanted to have his children and for us to have a family. When we first started dating, Cory told me that he wouldn't be able to have children because of his birth defect called Eagle Barrett Syndrome. A part of me was heartbroken because I didn't know how I would get my dream of being a mother. We realized that financially, we wanted to be doing better, and the risks to my health weren't worth a pregnancy. I was disappointed, and hearing more about friends who were starting families left me with a bit of envy. Then, I felt ashamed of being so envious. I know I'm not the only person in this world with fertility issues, but why does every part of my life have to be so difficult? For so long, I wanted to have a family of my own, and when you're young, you tend to believe things will just eventually work out, but now that I'm in my thirties, I know that's not so simple.

Cory and I talked about adoption, but we knew financially it wouldn't be realistic for us. Plus, I've heard horror stories of disabled women getting turned down for adopting babies because they are disabled. I even thought about surrogacy but gave up the idea once I looked at the price. As I get older, I do love the idea of having a little family of our own. I had a dream once that I had just given birth, and I was holding our baby girl. I woke up depressed and cried in my closet because the dream felt so real; it almost felt like my subconscious was mocking me. With age comes the question of whether Cory and I can be happy with just each other. Cory told me, yes, and I believe him. He's my best friend, and I could see us living a life together without children. But why do we have to? Why is everything so hard? I know that I probably sound whiny about this, but it's the one topic of my life that I give myself grace for. I met this incredible man, and I want a family with him, but I can't, and it's hard. We also discussed fostering, and I would love to do that. As a kid, I didn't always feel safe at home, so giving that safety to a child would be so meaningful.

There have been times when I do remember good memories with my mother. Not every second was filled with trauma. Growing up, reading was my favorite thing to do. I loved it; I read whatever book I could get my hands on at the library. Sometimes, my mom would find books for me at thrift stores. I devoured every The Babysitter's Club book she could find for me. But when she did have a small amount of money, we would go to Barnes & Noble, and I could pick out one book. I always went for the Dear America series. My mom would say, "One day, your books will be in Barnes & Noble, and I'll make sure it's right where people can see them." That helped plant the idea of being a professional writer in my brain. I would think about that moment when my mom got to see my books on shelves. But because of her mental health, I don't think that day will ever come.

I would love to have a child to share my love of reading with. It's such an important part of my life, and I think it helps children discover new worlds. Even when I'm having a rough day and really miss my mom, I still think about those bookstore dates we shared. I don't think I'll ever stop daydreaming about starting a family because, like I said, manifestation is real, and no matter how Cory and I become parents, I'll be extremely grateful.

Soleil

I grieve the baby girl from a dream
A dream that ended too soon
Soft curls
Baby's breath
Eyes that glistened like the moon

I grieve the child I held only once
Inside an empty hospital room
Soft curls
Baby's breath
The scent of spring blooms

I grieve the experience that was never mine
A name chosen but never spoken
Soft curls
Baby's breath
I named you Soleil because you were brighter than the moon

Wine and Cigarettes

Do you mind if I leave lipstick marks
underneath you
Let the cigarette ashes drop
onto the linen
Run my fingers through my greasy mane
Trace your lips
As I exhale your name
Light every candle
Let the wax hit my fingertips
Feel it harden over my nails
Do you mind if I have a second cup
Let me pour this time
Bordeaux out of a coupe
It's the only crystal we have
One more cigarette
For the ride later on
Tucked inside my pocket
White lighter inside
Ready to flicker
Sometimes I think it helps the pain
Remember to drive fast
Talk slow

Oranges with Salt

In the summertime, at my grandparent's apartment, I would sit in the living room watching The Wizard of Oz and play with my granny's porcelain figurines of little Black children. When it was time for a snack, my granny would give me cold orange slices with a sprinkle of salt. The sweet juice dripped down my chin as I devoured the slices. The salt made the citrus taste even stronger and the flavor more refreshing. My relationship with food is an odd one. Growing up there were times when food just wasn't around when we were with our mother. Sometimes, a week or longer would go by and the only thing we had was sugar water.

I learned early on the pain of a growling stomach and when we did have food, I would purposely only eat a part of my dinner and put the rest in the freezer for when we would not have anything to eat. I loved watching the Food Network channel with my mom and River. We would fantasize about our mom being a famous chef. She was an amazing cook and when we did have food in the house, she recreated recipes we saw on television. Mom's favorite chef was Ina Garten: she loved how she made her recipes easy to recreate. We always said one day mom would live in the Hamptons like Ina and cook for friends. I think because of the lack of food in our lives when we did get it, we indulged deeply. We savored every morsel. I never told anyone about the hunger because as far as I knew everyone dealt with hunger. My friends and I would talk about the "struggle meals" our mothers made the night before. It was such a common occurrence that it felt like the norm.

I was recently diagnosed with an eating disorder and even with my childhood food insecurity, it was still so weird for me to consider myself as someone who has an eating disorder. Having an eating disorder never really crossed my mind because I love food. I love trying new ingredients, and the disordered eating was so sporadic that I didn't even think about it being something serious. A part of me was also embarrassed. Eating disorders aren't discussed in the Black community. My whole life when I heard about eating disorders, I always imagined thin white girls. It didn't cross my mind that this could also affect other communities.

I also believe that not having food security as a child played a huge role in my disordered eating. I was seventeen when I was diagnosed with type 2 diabetes. I was so malnourished that my pancreas couldn't work properly because of the lack of food, which developed into diabetes. Of course, the doctors never knew about the food problems at home. They just looked at me as another Black girl with diabetes, so nothing was really investigated.

I instead was given a crash course in diabetes management. All I could think about was how I would manage my wheelchair, bladder issues, and now this new disease, all while doing well in my senior year of high school. I spent a lot of time obsessing over nutritional fact labels on food items, which caused my OCD to need every box in the house turned away from me, so I didn't see the (in my mind) threatening nutritional labels. I started not eating. I figured if I ate just a bit of food to be able to take the oral medication I was prescribed for the diabetes, I wouldn't have to worry about my glucose levels. At my appointments, the doctors were impressed with my A1C levels, which fueled the disordered eating.

I felt like I was losing out on life. Anthony Bourdain once said, "Meals make the society, hold the fabric together in lots of ways that were charming and interesting and intoxicating to me. The perfect meal, or the best meals, occur in a context that frequently has very little to do with the food itself." I felt like I wasn't really enjoying all that life could give to me. Food brought me so many happy memories in my life, like when my grandmother let me help her bake cakes as a little girl, giving me the spatula and bowl to lick once the cakes were in the oven. When food was available, I watched my mom cook in the kitchen—making everything from her Swedish meatballs to her berry muffins. I associated and still associate food and cooking with showing love. When Cory and I first got together, we bought a lot of cookbooks to try out new recipes together. I was excited to cook some of my favorite dishes for Cory as well. The first meal we made was lentil stew, which we found in a cookbook for learning the basics. That was almost six years ago, and we still use this recipe. Cooking is like a form of meditation for me. It brings me joy. I bought us a recipe box to hold all our handwritten recipe cards, so if we have children, we'll be able to pass them on.

I'm very grateful to live without the fear of starvation, and I'm grateful I recognized my disordered eating wasn't healthy for me. As far as my diabetes goes, I've been fortunate to have a great team of doctors, and I've been able to enjoy food without anxiety. My only hope is that I continue to grow and keep a healthy relationship with food. I'm so in love with trying new things that I'll try anything at least once. I even started growing my own herbs to really appreciate the effort and hard work it takes to bring something to life and nurture growth.

Not too long ago, I was in the kitchen fretting over some weight gain. I had to stop myself and tell myself kinder things. I grabbed a blood orange and sprinkled a bit of sea salt on it. I had not done that in years, but as I ate, I felt like that young girl again, not thinking about anything but the flavors I tasted. I knew I owed it to myself to really enjoy food and not worry about my body image. Something as simple as an orange with salt reminded me to look at food through the eyes of a child, unbothered.

Between Spring and Summer

You eat your oranges with a sprinkle of salt
Letting the juice run down your wrist
Droplets of sweat bead on your forehead
Wiping them away
Forgetting about the concealer you used to hide a blemish
The white sundress is low cut enough so the sun can linger on your cleavage
Dandelions tickle your ankles as you sway on the swing set
You pluck one from the ground
Lift it up to your lips
and blow
Making a wish to always feel like a carefree child
A wish for the sunset to wait.

My Two Great Bunny Loves

This essay originally appeared in the December 2023 issue of *Best4Bunny Magazine*.

I got Iggy in 2021 from a woman whose bunny had given birth. He was eight weeks old. When I first saw his big blue eyes and funny ears, I knew I needed him. This was a big deal for my husband and me because the summer before we lost our precious Bianca. Bianca was a jet-black Holland lop. I chose her because no one else wanted to adopt an all-black bunny from the rabbitry, especially since there were so many other brightly colored ones. She was very sweet but timid. Nevertheless, I immediately bonded with her. As a wheelchair user, I can't always get out of the house, and this was especially difficult during the COVID-19 pandemic. Having Bianca, there was a motivation for my mental health: she needed me and was so tiny and fragile. I felt like a mother and knew I had to put her needs before mine, which also helped me get up and do what self-care things I needed to do for myself so I could be available to her. She loved oats, and she loved lounging in the living room. Unfortunately, early in the morning, as we were getting ready for a trip, my husband discovered that Bianca had passed away. I broke down, screaming in his arms as he tried to comfort me. I had just pet her the night before, and she was fine. Losing her was so unexpected. I didn't know how I could go on without her. I vowed that I would never get another bunny. Bianca was right by my side when I wrote and published my first book; she always settled my anxiety, and now she was gone. At her funeral, I remember saying to her that I didn't understand why she left me when I still needed her.

It took me a while to even look at other bunnies, but once I found Iggy, this all-white fluff ball with blue eyes and ears that stuck out like airplane wings stole my heart. We settled on naming him Iggy after an anime character from our favorite show, *JoJo's Bizarre Adventures*. The character is a tiny dog who is super brave with a lot of sass. I'm so glad we chose that name, because it fit him perfectly. When his previous owner dropped him off at my house, I held him and fell in love and so did my husband. Later that night I noticed he hadn't used the bathroom yet. My husband and I both panicked and called the previous owner. She said that he was probably nervous and to put a stuffed animal with him. A month prior a friend who crochets stuffed animals made one for me that looked just like Bianca. I put the Bianca stuffy with Iggy. Immediately he snuggled up to her and started to lick her. Moments later, he was in his litter box. It was almost like Bianca's spirit was still helping me with my anxiety, and helping Iggy too.

I don't know why Bianca passed away so young, and for a long time I blamed myself. But rabbits are so fragile and rarely show any signs of pain because they are prey animals. She had a vet visit prior to her passing and was fine. But because of losing her I'm very cautious with Iggy. He really is like our child. I understand that I won't have him forever and I make the most of that by never forgetting to tell him what a good boy he is and how much I love him. I snap photos every chance I get; I regret not having many photos of Bianca.

I think it's important to give yourself time and grace when mourning the loss of a pet. They are your family, and grief takes many forms for different people. I'm thankful I gave love a second chance and found Iggy. Every day, he brings so much joy to our lives. I love that he's curious and affectionate. I love how brave he is; he doesn't hesitate to explore around the house. When we first got him, his favorite thing to do in our home office was jump and sit in the windowsill. This scared us so much that we rearranged the room to "Iggy proof" it because clearly just bunny-proofing wasn't enough for our little Olympian. I want rabbits to always be a part of my life. I joke that if I were an animal, I would want to be a bunny. I hope one day to have my own rescue and often dream of being able to save rabbits that people discard like trash. It breaks my heart to hear about rabbits who have been mistreated. How could anyone look at these tiny creatures and want to harm them? Right now, we don't have the finances or room to take care of more rabbits, but I continue to daydream and will hopefully manifest it. I truly believe it's what Bianca would want. She was so friendly and deserved so much more time. Opening a sanctuary to honor her would be my gift to her for helping bring me out of a depressive time in my life.

It's All Politics

I'll be honest: I debated including this in the book. Mainly because it still seems so unreal. I can honestly say that there has never been a time when I wanted to be a politician or work in politics. But somehow in the summer of 2021, I ended up on Dennis Kucinich's communications team for the Cleveland mayoral campaign. It was a wild ride, and I can finally talk about an experience that truly traumatized me.

A friend from high school, professional dancer Nehemiah Spencer, reached out to me to be a part of a video project that was celebrating Black Girl Magic. It was incredible and an amazing experience. The videographer took notice of me, especially after I mentioned the recent publication of my poetry collection. Unbeknownst to me, he was working with Dennis Kucinich to get a mayoral campaign going. I didn't know much about Dennis other than that he was once the youngest mayor of Cleveland in the 1970s and he broke a tooth on an olive pit in the House of Representatives cafeteria. The videographer, Michael, later told me he talked about me to Dennis and Dennis wanted me to be on his communications team for his campaign. Supposedly he was impressed with my background as a writer and valued my experience as a Black and disabled woman.

Michael and I were the only Black people on the campaign. Everyone else were white college-age kids. One girl was still a teenager. I was excited not because I saw a future in politics but because I saw this as a way to really help the local disabled community and fight for more accessibility around the city. Everyone had already been meeting, and I was the last to join the team. I joined my first Zoom meeting in the spring of 2021. Dennis let us know that he had a book coming out and he wanted us all to read it. The book detailed his time as mayor in Cleveland in the seventies and everything he did to fight the monopoly of utility companies. Michael dropped the book off at my house a week later. It was a proof copy that writers get before it's published. The book was almost seven hundred pages. I knew I would take a long time to get through it.

A few weeks into the campaign, Cory and I lost our bunny, Bianca. Her passing away unexpectedly really put me in the doldrums, so I threw myself into the campaign to keep my mind off things. I was an emotional wreck, crying randomly throughout the day, but I always pulled it together for our weekly campaign meetings. I was asked if I read the book. I lied and said yes, though I had barely glanced at the first chapter. As we got closer to having Dennis officially announce his candidacy, I became nervous about whether the policies I wrote for Dennis would help shape him into being a great mayor for the disabled community.

On June 14, 2021, in front of the Cleveland signature sculpture in Tremont, we held a press conference to announce his run for mayor. Every local news station was there with their camera ready, and reporters were standing by. Soon Dennis called me and everyone else up to stand beside him. I was nervous about the cameras, so I just tried to smile and not look awkward. I wasn't too worried about what Dennis would say because he was fairly liberal and nothing alarming caught my attention in the meetings leading up to this day.

However, as he began his announcement, I heard the words "four hundred" and "cops." He wanted to add four hundred cops to the city. I thought back to every meeting we had and didn't recall ever hearing this. It had been one year since the murder of George Floyd—the last thing the city needed was more cops. The lack of police wasn't the reason the city had issues. So many other things needed more attention, specifically homelessness and mental health care. I sat there with a smile plastered on my face trying not to show any alarm. My soul was crushed though. This wasn't something I agreed with. As a Black, disabled woman, I have always leaned towards more abolitionist views. I'm a firm believer in getting people the necessities they need and not turning to the prison system as the answer.

The sun was beating down on me and I didn't know how much longer I could sit and listen to the speech. Once it was over, I rushed home, upset, and confused. I was one of two Black people standing beside Dennis, and I felt like I had let my community down. I didn't want anyone to believe I shared those views. But another part of me told myself that I was doing this to make a name for myself as an activist and that working on this campaign was an experience for future opportunities. I also told myself that maybe I was being overly emotional because I was still grieving the sudden death of my sweet Bianca.

Dennis was relying a lot on him being a household name and whatever previous accomplishments he had as the "Boy Mayor" in the seventies. I started not seeing eye-to-eye with a couple of people on the campaign team because I felt like they were more interested in saying yes to every idea Dennis had instead of being honest, so we wouldn't be alienating certain demographics. When I started on the campaign, I thought my unique background of being disabled and Black would be utilized more, but unfortunately I felt like a prop more than anything. After the speech I figured things would calm down. But they didn't. I don't remember the exact date, but I remember it being Friday morning when I got a text telling us we needed to meet on Zoom right away. I had no idea what this could be about and was confused. Michael texted me, "Do you know what's going on?"

"No idea," I replied.

Soon Dennis, his wife, and the campaign manager all joined the call. They began talking about "the mailer," and I had no clue what they were talking about. I got on Twitter and was horrified to see a mailer that had been sent out by the campaign to Cleveland residents that pictured the iconic Cleveland script sculpture plagued with bloody bullet holes. I wanted to cry and most importantly I wanted to quit the campaign. Justin Bibb, who was also running for mayor, already voiced his anger over the mailer. His campaign was dragging us (rightfully) through the mud. We were Dennis's comms team, and we didn't know anything about this. If we had, it would not have gone out. At that moment I realized that no matter what we told Dennis, he was going to do what he wanted to do. I got off the call furious that this was happening. I felt like everyone was being delusional and not taking the complaints we were getting seriously. I was also embarrassed because again I felt like I was letting my community down.

Later that day I wrote in the group chat that Dennis had basically just told the city of Cleveland to fuck off. Someone in the group chat sent it to Dennis, and it wasn't long before I got an email from him saying we needed to talk. That night as I waited for Dennis to call, I couldn't help but wonder how I got into this situation. Not only was my mental health declining but my physical health was also not doing great. I think the stress of everything was too much for my body to handle. When he called, he asked me why I was so upset about the mailer. I told him truthfully: it was a big screw you to the city that he wanted to represent. I love Cleveland, it's my hometown, and it's not perfect, but we don't need our own leaders dragging it. Also, the depiction of gun violence triggered me. I grew up in not-so-safe neighborhoods on the east side of Cleveland, and gun violence was nothing to make light of. Scare tactics weren't going to change things. Mocking the city wasn't going to change things. To my surprise, after saying all of this through tears, Dennis apologized, but only for hurting me and not making the mailer. He stood by his decision, but he felt bad about me being hurt. I told him before getting off the phone that I needed to work on my mental health, and he told me he completely understood. I stopped going to meetings, and I took myself out of group chat. I only stayed in contact with Michael. In August of that year, I ended up getting so sick with a bladder infection that I ended up in the hospital for almost a week. Word got back to Dennis, and he called to check on me and talk to me so I wouldn't feel alone. He asked me if there was anything he could do to help, and I told him no, but that I really appreciated him calling to check on me.

The campaign moved on, and Dennis wasn't coming up strong as a leader in the polls. Justin Bibb ended up winning. I decided not to get involved in any more political campaigns, but one thing I am extremely grateful for is Dennis pushing me to go to a Clevelanders for Public Transit meeting. Early in the campaign, he wanted me to go to a meeting to see what issues the members were talking about. I never really thought of public transit as a form of activism, but I soon realized that my desire to be an advocate for the disability community had a lot to do with transit. Once I got better physically and mentally, I threw myself into Clevelanders for Public Transit. I felt like my background was being used to help and that I was making a difference. Soon, I was nominated to be on the board, and I took on the role of co-chair. Michael and I did not stay in touch; he blocked me on Twitter because he saw that I liked a tweet about defunding the police. That hurt because he had become such a dear friend and even spoke at Cory's and my commitment ceremony. But I wasn't going to back down on my views: people come into your life for a reason, but they don't stay every season, and that's okay.

I have no hard feelings towards Dennis. The experience is something I can tell my future kids about one day. A lot of people can't say they were on a political campaign, so that's sort of unique. Having that experience on my resume, plus my work with Clevelanders for Public Transit, made it possible for me to get my first real career job as a volunteer and activist coordinator for a nonprofit organization. I know a lot of people don't believe it, but I truly do believe the universe works to put you exactly where you need to be. It would be easy to dwell on the negative experiences, and for a little while, I did, but I decided to take them as learning opportunities. Though I still have absolutely no plans ever to be a politician, and I don't see that changing, Dennis once told me that what he liked about me was that I was sensitive. He said, "We need more people like you, Shalida," and I can't help but agree.

So Alone

I feel so alone
Dancing with a shadow
So misty
All on my own
Falling down slowly
Will anyone be there to catch me
Drifting in the wind
Please hold my hand
Come catch me
Only if you can
Spiraling towards the sea
My neck is straining
Underwater parades chase me away
I swim slowly
I touch the sand
Let it slip through my fingers
The scenery painted robin egg blue
Sadness never tasted so sweet

Sheltered

After becoming homeless and not being able to stay with granny, me, River, and mom ended up staying with my uncle and his wife in their cramped government-assisted apartment. There were three bedrooms and twelve people living in the house, most being my uncle and his wife's grandchildren. I knew from the beginning that this wasn't going to work out for us. My uncle's wife was controlling. Within a few weeks, she was already picking fights with my mom about silly stuff like not washing the dishes the right way.

My mom, River, and I spent most of our time in the upstairs bedroom, coming downstairs to eat dinner only when summoned.

The three of us shared a full-size bed. I was twenty-four and extremely depressed because yet again, I was struggling and facing hardship with my family. The only time we could eat was when my uncle's wife cooked for the kids, which was always late, and we had to sit at the table with the kids as she watched us.

After a couple of months being there and dealing with the emotional and sometimes physical abuse, I couldn't take it anymore. I was sick of living this way and I was sick of seeing my mom being bullied and not being able to stand up for herself. One night at dinner after a whole day of her nagging at my mom, I couldn't hide my outrage. My mom got up to wash the dishes and my uncle's wife yelled at her. I was pissed, I looked at her and rolled my eyes. Afterwards I went upstairs. The next morning my uncle texted my mom letting her know we were no longer welcome in his home since I disrespected his wife. I saw this as my opportunity to finally get us out of this situation. We had family therapy that morning and I encouraged my mom to talk to a case manager so we could get into a safe environment instead of going back.

Thankfully, we were able to get a spot in a domestic violence shelter in Geauga County far away from any urban life. We only had to pack up a few belongings and the case manager would take us to the new shelter. Getting our stuff turned out to be more dramatic than I expected—my uncle tried to throw my mother down a flight of stairs because she cried and begged him to forgive me for my actions. I didn't feel bad, and I was never going to apologize: it needed to be done, we needed to get out of there. Me rolling my eyes because she was barking orders at my mom didn't come close to the shit she put us through. My whole attitude was, "fuck these people, they don't care about us." As we stuffed everything into the case manager's small car, we headed into the unknown. Up to that point I had never been in a shelter before, and I was nervous. But I also felt relieved because at least I wasn't in an abusive household anymore.

Once we got to the shelter, I saw how truly secluded we would be. No one would be able to find us, and that thought alone gave me a bit of hope. As we got into the shelter, we were met by staff to do our intake process. Everyone seemed nice enough, though a lot of staff were my age, so I felt a bit self-conscious. It was a long day, and I just wanted to sleep. After intake, we were brought into the shelter and shown to our beds. Little kids ran around, and mothers tried to do normal "at home" tasks, like cooking and laundry. There was a big communal kitchen with two refrigerators and one deep freezer stocked with food. We were told we could put our own food into the fridges, but we were more than welcome to help ourselves to food that had been donated. Once we got to our beds, I immediately sunk into the bottom bunk. Mom started getting text messages from my uncle's wife that ranged from her making fun of my wheelchair to completely disrespecting my mom. I told my mom to block her.

That first night we slept surprisingly well—I think all our adrenaline wore off and we were able to crash. We got up the next morning and met with some staff members to learn more about the rules of the shelter. Everyone was expected to do chores, no eating in the living room, you can't keep your own medication (even insulin), and you cannot under any circumstances reveal where you were staying. The last rule was the most important because a lot of the women in the shelter were hiding from dangerous spouses. There was one last piece of advice the staff gave us: don't make friends. Everyone in the shelter is dealing with the same thing. It's probably the only thing we all have in common but even if you're building a connection, it's just trauma bonding. Besides, the goal wasn't to make friends, the goal was to get out of the shelter.

Despite the advice, we immediately became friends with a young Black mother and her two tween daughters. We were the only Black people in the shelter then, so we bonded immediately. The mother was escaping an abusive husband. My mom was about ten years older than her, and she really seemed to look at my mom as an older sister. We did our grocery shopping together; River and I babysat her daughters. We formed our own little group. There was another woman named Bea who was staying in the shelter for a third time. Her partner kicked her out and she made her way back to the shelter. She was young, only twenty-nine, but had already lost all her teeth. She told us she didn't have family, so she clung to us. She really befriended River and the two built a friendship.

I ended up celebrating my twenty-fifth birthday in the shelter. The local mall donated brand new clothes for me from Victoria's Secret and other stores; it felt like a real birthday. A guy I met on Tinder, who ended up becoming a good friend, picked me up from the secret pick-up location the shelter used and took me out to dinner at a Thai place. Afterwards, we hung out at a cemetery, just talking about where we saw the rest of our twenties going. I was honest when I told him I had no idea, and he agreed that he didn't know either. Before he dropped me off, he gave me a couple birthday gifts, some crystals, and a silver Tree of Life necklace "to keep you safe," he said.

For the first couple of months, things went well enough at the shelter. My mom got a job at a convent as a nurse's aide. All three of us were in therapy, and we were ready to start looking at a place of our own. But soon the dynamic of the shelter changed. A woman with severe mental health issues was brought to the shelter and on her first night, she spread her period blood on the chairs, put her cigarette ashes in the sugar jar, and would stand in the mirror screaming at nothing anyone could see. No one felt safe around her, especially the numerous little kids who were staying at the shelter. We brought this up to the director of the shelter and she blew off our concerns.

Not long after she arrived, a mom with her three young children and her best friend moved in. Immediately, we butted heads with the two women. They were racist. Bea started hanging out with them and revealed to them that she had a daughter across the country—something she never revealed to us. They would make an "all whites table," and when we brought it up to the majority white staff, we were told to be grateful we had a place to live. Soon, Bea had planned on bringing her five-year-old daughter, whom she had sent to live with a random couple, back to Ohio to be with her in the shelter. This alarmed us because she told River that a couple of years prior, she was arrested for being inappropriate with a minor girl. As soon as we found this out, we again went to the staff to voice our concern. We had so many young kids in the shelter, and we had a genuine concern for their well-being with Bea in the shelter. We were told to focus on our own journey. Soon, an obvious divide happened in the shelter; by the summer, there was a single Mexican mom of six and a Black single mom with three boys in the shelter with us. All the white people hung out together and made us feel uncomfortable.

One night, the white single mom with three kids and her best friend were making lobster and other shellfish in the kitchen. River has an extreme allergy to seafood. Because of this the shelter made it known that those items couldn't be cooked in the shelter. They made a huge mess as they cooked, leaving sauces and empty shells scattered around the kitchen. I knew River and I had kitchen duty that night and was worried about River going into anaphylactic shock. So, I went into the kitchen and asked them if they could clean up. They flipped out, screaming and getting into my face. My only thought was, "Please don't make me have to fight these bitches." I had so much built-up anger from the racism that was going ignored and the verbal threats from them with no consequences I started to feel myself boiling over. I made the decision to get a staff member. The staff member I got was a sweet, older white woman who taught crocheting to us. She made them clean and bleach the kitchen. Another staff member came and asked what was going on. I told her the situation. She said, "I'm not surprised. Hopefully, they get kicked out for this." I was surprised to hear that even some staff noticed how terrible they were.

The next morning, I was called in to meet with the director; she heard about the night before, and somehow, I became the villain. Even though I handled the situation the correct and safe way by getting a staff member, I was the one who got scolded like a child and told to mind my business. Well, that just wasn't going to work out because my sibling's well-being is my business, and I don't care if I have to fight a million racists I will always look out for River. Me, River, and Mom grew tired of the shelter and had saved enough to start looking around for our own place. I was trying to figure out ways to get back into blogging and make money doing it so I could help us get out faster. I called my friend JP, who I had met a year earlier at Disney World, for some advice on how to get back into social media. He could tell something was wrong in my voice. I broke down in tears and told him about us living in the shelter. He let me cry as much as I needed. He gave me some advice on how to get the blog moving again and told me he and his family would be praying for us. I really needed that.

Soon we found an affordable place to live in Geauga County. Moving out of the shelter was the best feeling. Leaving the people who caused me so much turmoil was an enormous weight lifted off my shoulders. I was also happy not to have anything else to do with the staff. Towards the end, they really showed their true colors. I ended up finding out the reason the mom and her best friend never got any consequences for being overtly racist was because they had a family member on staff—it all made sense. I did feel bad about leaving the Mexican mother because she was so kind. When she first arrived, she bought us a pizza to share. Her kids were sweethearts and always so kind. I also worried about Bea's daughter; we all grew attached to her when she arrived and worried about her safety, especially since the staff didn't listen to our concerns over Bea's criminal background. Bea also got her own apartment and would be moving with her daughter right after us.

We never quite settled into the new place. Geauga County was different from being in Cleveland. It was so rural, and where we lived, there weren't even sidewalks. I spent time writing and River spent time painting, and my mom's mental health began to decline because of the seclusion. People who we felt were close friends from the shelter all drifted apart. I understood then why they said not to make friends. We didn't have the trauma of shelter living to keep us together, so we all went our separate ways and tried to forget about that unfortunate time in our lives. A caseworker from the shelter would come out once a week to check on us and see if we needed any help with furniture or food. One day, she came by and told us that Bea had been arrested for kidnapping. She left her daughter with a stranger and took an Uber all the way from Ohio to Pennsylvania to pick up a thirteen-year-old girl, brought her back to Ohio, and had her in her apartment, assaulting her. Sadly, I wasn't completely shocked. We had told the shelter about her background, and they told us to mind our business. I never thought I would be in a shelter. I am happy that I made it out, though, and slowly, we all ended up leaving the house in Geauga.

I Am, I Am, I Am

I think the best part about life is how music, art, poetry, and people kind of shape you into the person you are. I got my first tattoo after completing my first writer's residency. I got the quote "I am, I am, I am" from *The Bell Jar* to mark the completion of the residency. I always loved the work of Sylvia Plath, and of course, I related to her struggles with mental illnesses. That quote got me through some of my darkest times. When I needed to center myself during an anxious situation, I would repeat that quote over and over until my mind was only focused on the words and not the anxious thoughts.

In Sylvia Plath's *The Bell Jar*, the main character Esther talks about the direction of her life with the analogy of a fig tree. Each branch is a possible direction her life could go in. That resonates with me because I believe every part of my life could have gone completely differently. A part of me wonders if one branch is the version of myself as a famous poet. She didn't chicken out when she got accepted into a university in New York City and made a name for herself. She spends her days writing and her nights drinking wine and listening to Frank Sinatra. She's confident in her looks and has a group of friends who are more like family.

Another one of my branches is the mother version of myself. I'm a mom and I have a husband who adores me. I spend my time taking care of my children. Watching them grow up and taking them on little adventures. They never have to fight for my love, and they never have to worry about food or shelter. I'm gentle with them and I give them my support no matter what. My husband and I aren't perfect and that's okay because we love one another and make sure our family is comfortable.

The next branch is what would have been the outcome if I went through with my suicide plan. Would I have succeeded? What happens when you die? Is there really an afterlife? I can imagine my family and close friends being hurt by my passing but besides that I know eventually everybody dies; after all I'm only a small dot on a giant rock. On a twig of that branch, I survived and was put into a mental health facility. That's probably what I needed. I would've gotten help earlier and created a mental health plan that made it a lot easier to live. I didn't feel desperate for love and affection because loving myself was enough. I wouldn't have to pop a Xanax every time some bitch used racial microaggressions against me.

There's a branch where I'm a famous songwriter and I get to work with my heroes Kid Cudi, Fiona Apple, and Lana Del Rey. I write songs that people listen to at three in the morning when insomnia is kicking their ass and all they have to keep them going are my lyrics that soothe their souls. I love to daydream about what my life could have been, but I understand there's a point where that becomes unhealthy.

Now here's a branch that is the life I have. I have an amazing husband who loves every part of me, even the parts I haven't figured out how to love yet. I have a couple friends who are more like family, and on stressful workdays I do put on my Frank Sinatra record and pour a glass of wine to feel like the bad bitch that I know I am. I get to wake up feeling incredibly loved, not just in my romantic life but from the family I created for myself. I used to think I would never get the chance to wake up and feel loved. Through years of therapy, I finally know deep down that I'm capable of being loved. Even on the darkest days, I still know that love is what I should expect from myself and those I choose to have around me.

I'm amazed with the growth I've forced myself into. Growing up I was so hard on myself when it came to how I viewed myself. I was, like many people, my biggest critic. Never giving myself enough credit. I'm not sure if it was just the disability or the combination of being a little Black girl in America that made me feel like I wasn't good enough. I was also taught at a young age not to be "conceited," which meant not complimenting myself or celebrating my victories. I also believe the lack of self-love was a mirror of my mother. She was very self-deprecating, and I took on those habits. My mother didn't love who she was and in turn I learned that I couldn't love who I was. Of course, it's not fair to put that all on my mother because she too was once a little Black girl in America with a disease (diabetes) that back in the seventies and eighties (and even now) had a racist stereotype attached to it.

I'm trying every day to give enough to love myself that I heal that little girl I once was. Whatever love is left I plan to give it to my mother's inner child. I think if she had had love, a lot of things would have turned out so differently. Cory tells me all the time that I love love. And he is so right. Love is one of the things that keep me going and I think deep down everyone is a lover of love. Since I am a person that loves love I still believe in fairytales. The first books I remember reading as a child were fairytales. I dreamt of having my own love to share a castle with. As an adult, I've come to terms that fairytales can exist and not be perfect, and that's completely okay. Not every day will be filled with happiness and not every day will go smoothly. It's how you get through those rougher days that define your personal fairytale.

What worked for me was to accept myself as the heroine of my story; to see myself as a queen. It's easy to want others to view you that way but when it comes to seeing yourself in that light, it can be difficult. I gave myself permission to love myself and in turn, developed self-confidence. If I hadn't, I really don't think I would have ended up in a relationship that was healthy. In my past relationships, I didn't think highly of myself, so I didn't correct people when they treated me badly.

My relationship with Cory is far from perfect. Mainly because we're both flawed individuals. In my twenties, I assumed if a relationship wasn't perfect it wouldn't work. It's not a bad thing that I needed to change my expectations; it was realistic. You can still believe that you'll have your own fairytale and also know that perfection doesn't exist, but I get to wake up next to a man who values my thoughts, is considerate of my feelings, and is patient with me. That to me is the most perfect imperfect fairytale.

I'm also very fortunate to be able to give love to my furry babies. I always loved animals, even when I was younger. There's something so pure about them. They put their lives in your hands because they trust you and I think that's so magical. I grew up with cats but after meeting Cory we had to think of animals that didn't bother his allergies. Somehow two chinchillas fell into our laps. Matzoball and Latkes. Two fluffballs full of personality. I never had my "own" pet growing up but always dreamed that one day I would. Now I have the chinchillas and my rabbit, Iggy. Caring for any animal lights up my life. It makes me feel like a better human and that's all I'm really striving for. I don't aim for perfection—just the ability to look in the mirror and be proud of the woman I am and give myself credit for my accomplishments.

I've been building the life I wanted for a while now, and it still feels like a dream come true. I have Cory, who is truly my best friend, the cutest animals, and a new career as a volunteer coordinator for a non-profit, which is something I thought I wouldn't be able to have. I am proof that you don't need a fancy degree to shine in life. I didn't have a college degree, but I had experience, I had a story, and I had dedication. You can make it by just being you. So maybe I'm not wealthy but this life is all I ever really wanted when I really think hard about it.

I also try to heal the parts of my life that traumatized me when I was younger. I was nine when I quit ballet. I became extremely insecure about my wheelchair and the way I looked. I always thought about revisiting ballet to heal that little girl in me. I recently decided to sign up for adult classes and I'm so proud of myself. I'm not doing it to be the best or to be perfect, I'm doing it for fun and joy I once remember having as a little girl. Having an eating disorder and body dysmorphia doesn't make that an easy ask. Every day is a battle, but I cherish the days when my thoughts aren't flooded with food or weight loss or nitpicking every "flaw" in my body. I'm getting older and I appreciate good health more than the constant worry of getting curvier. Growing older and wiser is truly a better gift than anything else.

With learning to love myself I'm also learning to forgive myself for the unkind things and words I've said to myself. I'm learning to be more vulnerable because I've learned that's the only way to really form a deeper relationship with yourself and let others in. I'm learning to trust my decisions and not to second-guess myself so much. The whole world will try to gaslight you; you don't need to be doing it to yourself. Every day in every way I'm becoming better and better.

The Lore of Me

Like bones that are passed down
one generation to the next
until they come together and put together
a skeleton.

Stories whispered from person to person
glances throughout the room
These people only have seen one bone of me
I'm not complete for them

Here is the creation of the lore of me

Glitter on the Floor

People would love me
If I were a pretty poet
Glitter on the floor
Drinks passed around
Celebrating the words
I put on paper
Ears stretching to hear
Every gentle syllable I whisper
Champagne bottles overflowing
Eyes following me as I sway to the stage
A gold pen I use to loop my name on a book
Cameras flashing
All eyes on me

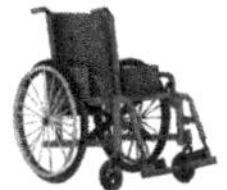

Acknowledgments

If you have this book thank you for reading it. I know a lot of it wasn't easy to read, so I appreciate you wanting to learn more about my life. When I set out to write this book, I immediately knew I needed to make sure my acknowledgments included those most important to me and those who helped me reach this huge goal in my career. Never in a million years would I have imagined I would be writing my memoir in my early thirties. What a ride it has been.

Funny enough, this book wouldn't exist if it wasn't for the Clevelanders for Public Transit. Thank you, Adam Bresnahan, for encouraging me to submit my work to The Pilgrim Press.

It still blows my mind at how a simple conversation of us talking about my writing led to a book deal. Thank you to The Pilgrim Press for seeing my talent and being so accommodating—I can't wait to see what future stuff we work on together. For you, I will be forever grateful. For everyone else at CPT, Chris Martin (not that Chris Martin), Nat Ziegler, Chris Stocking, and everyone else, thank you for supporting me while I took a break from public transit advocacy to live my dream. I am extremely thankful for your support. Also, another thanks to Chris Stocking and his partner Mollie who took care of me on a road trip to Indiana to learn how to become a better anarchist. That was such a meaningful experience for me.

Thank you, Raechel Anne Jolie, for your support and for allowing me to join your retreat for writers. I wrote "My Religion" that weekend and I don't think I could have done it without the space you gave me. Niki Takesh, thank you for being such a great friend. Before my thirtieth birthday, I messaged you scared and sad that I wasn't moving in the right direction. You settled that fear in me, and I owe you so much for that. Kylie Koch, my best friend, my bridesmaid, my rock, I can't even begin to tell you how incredibly glad we're still friends all these years later. Thank you for supporting my wildest dreams and understanding when I'm too overwhelmed to check-in. I think everyone should have a Kylie of their own, but I'm glad you are mine. Mya and Jeff Koch, thank you for making me my best friend, and thank you for being a second set of parents to me. Your kindness does not go unnoticed. I love you guys.

Granny and Grandpa, thank you for always supporting me and cheering me on from day one. I love you two so much. My mother-in-law Karen Gil, and father-in-law Jeff Askanazi, thanks for making Cory (he's awesome), and of course, I'm extremely grateful for the kindness, advice, and support you two have shown me these last few years. Especially you Karen, I hit the mother-in-law jackpot.

River, I am so happy to have you in my life. Thank you for being the loudest cheerleader in my corner. I hope this book brings you a sense of peace about how we grew up. I don't know what I did to deserve such an incredible sibling. I can't wait to see everything you're going to do to make the world a better and cooler place. You're a rock star, and everyone should try to be more like you. Your patience, loyalty, and kindness bring me such joy.

Cory, the love of my life. My best friend. If I have you by my side, I have everything I need. I can't wait to experience the adventures we'll go on and how our little family will grow. Thank you for dealing with my sometimes crankiness and need for extra cuddles before bed. You never make me feel like I'm asking for too much, and that is why I'm so deeply in love with you.

Mom, I don't know if you will ever read this book and if you do, please understand that this is how I heal through my pain like I always did growing up. I wish we hadn't missed out on so many memories and years. I love you and I'm optimistic about the new relationship we are building.